THE
STORY
OF THE
IRISH
PEOPLE

THE
STORY
OF THE
IRISH
PEOPLE

SEAN O'FAOLAIN

AVENEL BOOKS
NEW YORK

Thanks are due to Mrs. W. B. Yeats for permission to include the late W. B. Yeats' poem *The Unappeasable Host;* and to Mr. Padraic Colum and The Macmillan Company for the use of his poem *I Shall Not Die for Thee* and to The Viking Press for permission to reprint passages from *The Silver Branch.*

This 1982 edition is published by Avenel Books, distributed by Crown Publishers, Inc. , by arrangement with the Devin-Adair Company, original publishers of this work.

Manufactured in the United States of America

Originally published as THE IRISH: A CHARACTER STUDY

Library of Congress Cataloging in Publication Data

O'Faoláin, Seán, 1900–
    Story of the Irish people.

    Originally published as: The Irish. Old Greenwich,
Conn. : Devin-Adair, 1949.
    1. Ireland—Civilization.   I. Title.
DA925.038   1982   941.5   82-1827
                                AACR2

ISBN: 0-517-379899

h g f e d c b

CONTENTS

*History proper is the history of thought.
There are no mere events in history.*

R. G. COLLINGWOOD

Explanation

THIS BOOK IS NOT a history of political events, although some political events are described briefly in the course of the main narrative. It is, in effect, a creative history of the growth of a racial mind; or one might call it a psychological history; or, if the term were not far too large and grandiose, the story of the development of a national civilisation; although what has happened to the Irish mind is not an undisturbed local expansion but a complex process of assimilation at the end of which Ireland enters, with her own distinctive qualifications, into the great general stream of European culture.

Irish readers will have become so accustomed to another approach—the nationalist concept, almost wholly a political concept, of Ireland always on the defensive against foreign enemies—that they especially might, without this preliminary explanation, be a little taken aback at a record which looks at Nationality solely from the viewpoint of Civilisation; which, for example, is interested almost exclusively in the great *gifts* brought to Ireland by the Norman invasion; which sees in the impact of all foreign influences not a political or even a military battle-ground but the battle-ground of a racial mind forced on each new occasion to struggle afresh with itself. Indeed, if this little

book were not intended for the widest audience I might
have dispensed with politics and war entirely, or merely
referred without details, and in passing, to such tiresome
events as invasions, reigns, parliaments, the rise and fall
of dynasties, all of which can have no interest for anybody
apart from what they contribute—generally without knowing it—to the sum of human civilisation.

A word of self-excuse. Books like Trevelyan's *English
Social History* are unknown for Ireland. All our histories
are nationalist, patriotic, political, sentimental. I have
not a single book to turn to which is not either pre-
occupied with the national ego and a delusion of its self-
sufficiency, or else a cursive record of political events, or
a source-book of these events. I know only two books on
Irish history—apart, of course, from specialised scholarly
works—that hack a clear perspective through the tangled
jungles of futile and pointless raids, counter-raids, battles,
sieges, 'victories' (over what is never otherwise made
clear), and so forth: those are Edmund Curtis's one-
volume *History of Ireland,* and Bishop Mathew's *The
Celtic Peoples and Renaissance Europe.* These are civilised books. I have made acknowledgment, here and there
in the text, to one or two special studies that have also seen
the local story in a larger perspective. But, otherwise, this
inadequate attempt at the interpretation of the Irish mind
in labour has had to be, in its small and—nobody knows
better than I—inadequate way, a pioneering effort, a hit
or miss affair of instinct rather than knowledge. Some
day somebody may write an 'Irish Social History' and
give a quite different value to events.

In one place I have used the image of the signpost when
speaking of an historical event, saying that it points for-

ward to a modern development. That will at once reveal
the weakness of all such essays as this. How do I know
what the inscription on each signpost is? Only by looking
back at it from the modern destination. But how do I
know what this modern destination is? It is all very well
for me to say—'There you can see Irishmen at a milestone
in their journey to what they have become to-day.' Who
am I to say what the Irish mind is like to-day? I can say,
'Circumspice.' But one has only to be in Ireland for two
days to know that the most popular Irish entertainment is
to circumspect, and to disagree. The validity, then, of this
book is largely a matter of its persuasiveness and credi-
bility. There will always be a variety of historical explanations for modern achievements and failures (in themselves interchangeable words according to points of view).
As the late R. G. Collingwood would have said, the truth
of the answers will depend always on the questions which
one asks. I hope I am at least clear as to my paramount
question: which is, to ask at every stage, 'What has this
event or this contributed—with whatever racial colouring
is no matter—to the sum of world-civilisation?' Where
I could see nothing of that nature emerge it seemed to
me that the event was barren and I ignored it. Since, for
these reasons, this little sketch ignores most of the incidents which are emphasised in our history-books, and is,
indeed, concerned not with incidents but with intelligence, it will seem to some far too simple a story. History,
however, is often simpler than the historians make it.

In the first section I describe the raw material of the
Irish nature or 'genius'; in the second, how intelligence
begins to burgeon under stress; in the third, the five representative types which have branched from these origins—

the peasantry, the Anglo-Irish, the rebels, the priests, and the writers. There is a sixth type which I have barely hinted at, the new middle-classes, or native bourgeoisie: they are the peasant in process of development or final decay, it is too soon to say which.

I · THE ROOTS

Political History

c. 300 B.C. to *c.* A.D. 500

The Celts invade Ireland. The period dealt with in the great imaginative histories and romances.

Establishment of local states, and the beginning of regionalism or particularism.

The arrival of Christianity (fourth century) and beginnings of monasticism.

The development of the social system described in the 'Brehon Laws.'

The Great Gods Die

IF WE TURN to early Irish literature, as we naturally may, to see what sort of people the Irish were in the infancy of the race, we find ourselves wandering in delighted bewilderment through a darkness shot with lightning and purple flame. One expects the beginnings of any people to be dark; the darkness at the beginning of the story of the Irish mind is an unnatural darkness. There is somewhat too much of the supernatural about it. Alternatively we may feel that here a racial imagination has, from the start, got out of control; or we may simply say that early Irish literature is wildly romantic; or that the popular idea of the Celt as a romantic is correct; or that the nineteenth century, in exploiting this romantic quality, committed only the fault of piling on top of something already sufficiently embroidered by nature a lot of superfluous William Morris trappings. But the impression of a supernatural infusion is, I think, far and away the most important one.

The Celt's sense of the Otherworld has dominated his imagination and affected his literature from the beginning. So I see him at any rate struggling, through century after century, with this imaginative domination, seeking for a synthesis between dream and reality, aspiration and experience, a shrewd knowledge of the world and a strange reluctance to cope with it, and tending always to find the

3

balance not in an intellectual synthesis but in the rhythm of a perpetual emotional oscillation.

This is to anticipate, and in this book I shall oscillate a great deal myself between the past and the present, ringing one against the other, which is the disadvantage as well as the only way of writing the psychological history of a people. For the moment I must presume that my reader will have some knowledge of early Celtic literature. The great tales must be well known, Deirdre and Conchubar, Cuchulainn and Emer and Fand and Etain, Diarmuid and Grainne, Oisin and Fionn. The modern romantic poets who have made them popular have sinned only in softening their starkness and decorating their decoration. But the gods do whistle in the air, appear and vanish, hover, shimmer through a veil, the Otherworld is always at one's shoulder and the sense of poetry is everywhere, though not always tamed to its purpose and never, outside the lyrics to which we must return later, winnowed of its chaff.

Magic and History

I will mention, very briefly, one run from one example to remind the reader of the highly imaginative quality of Celtic invention—the end of the piece called 'The Second Battle of Mag Tured' from the history book called *The Book of Invasions*. It depicts the end of the war between the people known as the Tuatha De Danaan and the Fomorians, who held them in bondage. It begins with the entry into the subject Nuada's palace, at Tara, of a warrior called Lug Lamfada, or Lugh of the Long Arm, whose prowess is so great that Nuada considers how to use him against the Fomorians. The passage which follows lifts us at once out of the world of history:

Thereafter the wizards of Ireland were summoned to them and their medical men and charioteers and smiths and farmers and lawyers. They held speech with them in secret. Then Nuada enquired of the sorcerer whose name was Mathgen what power he could wield. He answered that through his contrivance he could cast the mountains of Ireland on the Fomorians, and roll their summits against the ground. And he declared to them that the twelve chief mountains of the land of Erin would support the Tuatha De Danaan, to wit, Slieve League and Denna Ulad and the Mourne Mountains, and Bri Ruri and Slieve Bladma and Slieve Snechta and Slieve Mish and Nefin and Slieve Maccu Belgadan and Segais and Cruachain Aigle . . .

And the lochs of Ireland would dry before them and all the great rivers, but the Tuatha should drink as they needed. Then we hear of the Dagda, and Ogma, and the three gods of the Danaan people, and a plethora of themes enters with more magical servants, on both sides, including the Fomorian demigod, Balor of the Evil Eye:

An evil eye had Balor the Fomorian. That eye was never opened save on a battle-field. Four men used to lift up the lid of the eye with a polished handle which passed through its lid. If an army looked at that eye though they were many thousands in number, they could not resist a few warriors . . .

But Lug, so soon as Balor's eye was opened, cast a sling-stone right through the eye, and that stone passed through Balor's head and killed twenty-seven Fomorians. Indeed, so many were slain in that battle that they could never be reckoned 'until we number the stars of heaven, sand of sea, flakes of snow, dew on lawn, hailstones, grass under feet of herds, and the horses of Manannan Mac Lir (the waves) in a storm at sea.'

A Much-used Palimpsest

As one reads these elaborations—in, I repeat, an alleged historical record—the mind cannot help being a little dazed. As we shall see presently there is one other paramount reason for this besides the immediate spectacle of imagination drowning in its own excess, or besides the natural difficulty of then-thinking into times so remote: that paramount reason being our comparative ignorance of the mythological, or religious, back-references hidden in these heroic inventions. And before we come to that we must advert to a further and purely mechanical reason for a sense of confused bewilderment. We do not read the literature as it was originally created. The Christian scribes and the patriotic ficto-historians have freely altered the original records and the traditional lore to suit their own ends, so that what we read to-day is a much-used palimpsest, and it is the delight and agony of modern scholars to try to peel off the second, third, fourth, and, for all we know, four-hundredth retelling in order to expose the original thought. Not that the original thought, if it ever could be discovered, would itself be firmly stated. The early Irish shaped their notions of this life, and the other life, at a stage in their development when they had passed far beyond savagery but had not yet arrived at civilisation: that stage in human development when man's concepts are still fluid and formative, as well as when the arts of literature and design, which would have fixed the forms and attributes, for example, of their gods cannot keep pace with the imagination in labour. We Irish had no primitive Homer to shape our early, half-formed ideas into a connected whole, and the winds of time and latter-day piety have further blown these earliest dreams like smoke in wind about the sky. Myth and history, dreams and facts, are forever inextricably commingled.

Primitive Religion

It is therefore impossible to form any clear picture of the religious background of this primitive Ireland. Gods and demigods abound. The hierarchy is not to be codified. All one can say, and even that debatably and daringly, is that the great Jove of the Celts was the Dagda, which simply means the Good Father, also called the Oll Athair or All Father, the god of the Otherworld, and that he was primarily a sungod; though, as one might expect from so mighty and central a deity, he had many functions and aspects and many names, and many off-shoots, or doublets, or imitators, or demigods born of his endlessly procreative plasma. Had Christianity not intervened it is likely, at least it was possible, that these recreations from the one great archetype and primitive myth would have developed characteristics and lives of their own, and the end might have been a coherent Celtic pantheon. As it is, the scholars, coming on these vaguely characterised creatures —part god, part hero, partly humanised, partly 'explained' —can only assume that *Aed Alainn* (The Lovely Aed), or *In Ruad Rofhessa* (The Red and All-wise One), or *Goll* (The One-eyed), and scores beside, are all born of the one adoration. It is even held that the name of Ireland, *Eriu,* modern Irish *Eire,* is that of a sun-goddess.*

The attributes of the parent Dagda, Good Father, sun-god, or Otherworld-god, are, at any rate, clearly consonant with sun-worship. He is of enormous size; he rules the weather and the crops; he is swift; he wields a deadly club, which may be lightning; he owns a cauldron as inexhaustible as the cornucopia, and he is thought then to preside over the feasts of the Otherworld; he is very old and very wise, indeed he is the source of all wisdom, especially of occult wisdom. So must the Dagda have seemed, variously, as occasion suggested, to the early Irish.

The Great Gods Die

Let us see an example of how time has treated these early gods. 'It was natural,' says Professor O'Rathaille, 'to attribute great age and great knowledge to the deified sun, the heavenly eye who has observed the doings of countless ages of men.' It may be part of an early and simultaneous totemism that this sungod is thought able to assume the shape of animal or bird, such as the horse or the eagle who fly so swiftly and beautifully through the air. Elsewhere the animal who pre-eminently symbolises the powers of the netherworld has been the serpent; but there are no serpents in Ireland and one alternative transformation of the sungod chosen by the Irish was the salmon. (This folk-practice of replacing any item which is not locally feasible by one which *is* locally feasible is wide-

---

* In all this section I obediently follow the latest and most scholarly book on the subject—*Early Irish History and Mythology,* by Professor Tomás O'Rathaille. (Institute of Advanced Studies. Dublin, 1946. 21s.)

spread: e.g. in inland countries a folk-hero cannot descend
into the sea but can descend a lake or a well, and some
far-travelled story about him will, accordingly, be altered
in this respect.) Now this Salmon of Knowledge is well
known in Irish tales. They locate him, with due local patriotism, in various rivers, including the River Boyne,
which is presided over by one of the various equivalents
of the Dagda in human form, a hero named Elcmaire. In
an anecdote from the great Ulster, or Cuchulainn cycle,
Cuchulainn—the central Irish hero—attempts to catch
this Salmon of Wisdom and is opposed by Elcmaire, i.e.
Dagda, or God.

Therein the Celt is dualistically thinking of the gods
as, at one and the same time, beneficent and maleficent.
The gods possess wisdom, but the gods also guard their
wisdom: to win it man must fight the gods. But it is not
so stated—for the god is depicted as a human hero guard-
ing his second self-transformed into a salmon. The listeners to the tale would only partly perceive the divine truth
behind the mortal tale. As time passed the mortal tale
would come more and more into the foreground; the
primitive belief would fade; in the end, the great gods
would die.

Gods into Men

Nevertheless, although rationalisation, changes of no-
menclature, euhemerisation due to Christian distaste for
the old beliefs, might actually improve the elementary
myth, even alter it to great artistic advantage, behind
the veil it is the elementary myth which still dominates
and excites the imagination. We, however, having lost

the primitive key to the primitive gate, must be content
to read the tales purely as mortal tales. We may take them
as shimmering reflections of the primitive Celtic mind,
but we must not think of them as its pure creations.
They are, rather, the recreations of the civilised Celt
many, many centuries after the passing into oblivion of
the magnificently barbaric world which first set the wheel
of wonder into movement.

There is a very pleasant example of the skill with which
the Christian adaptors transformed the gods not merely
into mortal heroes but into those new demigods—the
saints. It occurs in Muirchu's *Life of Saint Patrick*. Here
Saint Patrick thunders against sun-worship, declaring that
all who adore the sungod will perish; but the Sun whom
he worships shall endure for ever, and all who adore Him
abide with Him for ever. Patrick is opposed by one Coll,
or Goll, meaning The One-eyed, which is a common
image for the sun; later this Coll becomes MacCuill, the
Son of Coll, and gradually MacGuill, Maguil, and Machaldus. This man plans to murder Patrick. But Patrick by his
own great miraculous power so astonishes his enemy that
he becomes converted and, as a penance, Machaldus is set
adrift in a rudderless and oarless coracle which bears him,
ultimately, to the Isle of Man. There pious tradition made
him into a Manx saint—Saint Maughold. It is a transformation of sun into saint which is not alone illustrative of
the process by which pagan god becomes Christian hero
but, also, of the infusion of pagan mythology into Christian
hagiography. The early Irish mind is, apparently, as fer-
tile when creating miracles as myths, though rarely as
graceful. The imaginative dominance is not, at any rate,
lessened by the arrival of Christianity.

Historical Fakes

We must see, too, how the historians worked their will on the gods. The most elaborate of their works is that great volume known as *The Book of Invasions,* a twelfth-century text, but doubtless begun several centuries earlier. The nineteenth-century scholars, such as Eugene O'Curry, took this volume as more or less genuine history; it is a measure of modern Irish scepticism that its latest critic roundly describes it as 'a deliberate work of fiction.' Its compilers set out to do several things; first, to explain, with considerable imaginative power, how it was that a variety of people seemed to have settled, from time to time, in this now supposedly purely 'Gaelic' island (the Goidels or Gaels were the last wave of Celtic invaders) ; second, to unify the country politically by giving all the contemporary upper classes a common Gaelic origin; thirdly, they set out with 'the deliberate intention of reducing the faded deities of pagan Ireland to the status of mere mortals.'

One of the finest inventions of these pious frauds was one completely imaginary invasion by those folk whom we have already met in 'The Battle of Mag Tured'—the Tuatha De Danaan—the word *dana* apparently means artistic skill of any kind. Thereafter, if, for example, the people of the wild, mountainous south-west looked on the two great rounded hills against the horizon which, to this day, are called the Two Breasts of Dana, it was hoped that they would see in these mighty prostrate paps not some ossification of a monstrous heathen goddess but some fanciful image related to these (imaginary) mortal colonists. And all the gods and all the demigods

would likewise be referred to this human origin, explained
and demoted.

Gods into Hobgoblins

But though a racial imagination may be tamed or dis-
ciplined (and these redactions are primitive efforts to do
this), it cannot be explained away into insensibility. If
one could personify it one might imagine it saying obsti-
nately, 'No, no! If to believe is sinful, to half-believe is
but a fancy. We will not reason the gods out of existence.
We will dream them into demigods and fancy them where
they may live in immortal peace.' So, in the sagas the
demigods abound, come and go, do not die but hide deep
in the earth, in marvellous palaces known as *side*—pronounced *shee*—and if the curious asked later where these
shee were, then men would point to the great burial
mounds, such as Brugh na Boinne, those vast tumuli which
may still awe the modern traveller at Knowth, Dowth and
New Grange. Two of them have been opened and show
great mortuary chambers, that at New Grange, one of the
largest in western Europe, now empty. (Even so did the
Greeks attribute their prehistoric monuments to the Cy-
clops.) This word *side* became, still later, transferred
from these 'palaces' to their occupants. In modern Gaelic
it has come to mean what we call the fairies. And there,
indeed, the great gods have at last died, not by being humanised but by being reduced to the status of elves, wood-
nymphs, hobgoblins, brownies, local Lares, poor remnants
of a great myth. In our day to give any credence even to
these displeases the clergy. The country folk talk of them
nowadays hardly at all. They tend, I think, to speak only
of what they call the *sprid*, the spirit, or ghost, a frighten-

ing and rather malevolent element; and, in any case, Irish
'fairy stories' as gathered from the people have never had
much of the dainty or sparkling or pretty about them.
Awe has remained to the end.

Hobgoblins into Poetry

It was this mingled and confused memory that Yeats
gathered into such poems as *The Unappeasable Host*:

The Danaan children laugh, in cradles of wrought gold,
And clap their hands together, and half-close their eyes,
For they will ride the North when the ger-eagle flies
With heavy whitening wings and a heart fallen cold;
I kiss my wailing child and press it to my breast
And hear the narrow graves calling my child and me.
Desolate winds that cry over the wandering sea;
Desolate winds that hover in the flaming West;
Desolate winds that beat the doors of Heaven and beat
The doors of Hell and blow there many a whimpering
    ghost;
O heart the winds have shaken, the unappeasable host
Is comelier than candles at Mother Mary's feet.

He has kept various strands—the power of the Otherworld beings to carry off children and leave changelings
in their place, their trick of appearing as birds or animals,
their dwelling under the earth, their malevolence, their
beauty. His poem is an interweaving of centuries upon
centuries of bright imaginings and dim rememberings, of
irrational terror and delight.

It was his immense good fortune to be born into an
Ireland where that traditional memory still flourished,
and so to see her as an ancient land, old as Judaea and
Egypt, with an ancient soul and an ancient aura, to find

in her people a great dignity and a great simplicity and a great sense of wonder. Out of it all he created an aesthetic based on the instinctive life of the soul and the passionate life of the body as against such destructive things as cold character and sterile knowledge that generalises all spontaneous life away into abstractions. He saw a folk-Ireland which is, even yet, far from dead though, like its beliefs, it now lives, as it were, underground.

Epic or Romance?

Our first approach to the early Irish world, through its literature, is thus a bewilderment not only because of its own imaginative richness but because of a deliberate mingling of history, myth, legend and religion—possibly our ancestors' first effort to synthesise an imaginative concept of life with their actual experience of it. It may have been this mingling (though he may not have fully appreciated its disintegrating effects) that forced one of the most sensitive as well as intelligent British scholars who ever examined Irish literature, the late W. P. Ker, to assert that the Celt never could create an epic—his genius was for Romance. Epic Ker defined as 'great actions in narrative with the persons well-defined'; that is, tales marked by their weight and solidity rather than by their mystery and fantasy, tales of men striving for human ends by their own right hands, tales from which the ultimate emergence was their human dignity rather than the adventitious dignity of semi-divinity or semi-historicity. He goes on:

'Many nations, instead of an Iliad or an Odyssey, have had to make shift with conventional repetitions in praise of chieftains, without any story; many (he is here referring to

early Irish literature) have had to accept from their story-
tellers all sorts of monstrous adventures in place of the
humanities of debate and argument. Epic literature is not
common. . . . The growth of the true epic is a progress
towards intellectual and imaginative freedom.'

This interior struggle towards 'intellectual and imaginative freedom' goes on in every race. The struggle
between the myth and the human drama is apparent even
in the Iliad and the Odyssey, though Ker is surely right
in saying that when, at the end of the Odyssey, silence
falls on the listeners it is the silence of admiration for the
narrator rather than wonder at his exploits. This is a
matter of proportion. All wonder has gone out of such
Saxon pieces as *The Fight at Maldon;* what remains is
an eroded human interest. A choking superabundance of
wonder dims the human figures in the Celtic sagas. The
scribes who tried to humanise Gods into credible heroes,
were, in so far, moving towards intellectual freedom;
when they turned them into incredible saints, they were
moving backwards again into intellectual slavery; when
the scribes were ficto-historians they were, quite simply,
selling their mythology for a mess of patriotic pottage.

Old Irish Humor

So, as we now have it, what pleases us most in the great
central saga of *The Tain Bo Cuailgne,* or *The Driving
Away of the Bull of Cooley,* are those runs in which defin-
able characters emerge, such as the unwilling fight between Cuchulainn and his dear boyhood friend Ferdia,
or the amusing incident of the wooden sword. I will re-
capitulate this last incident to show the style of this old
Irish humor. Fergus, it will be remembered, is a doubt-

ful ally of Queen Maeve and her husband Ailill in their Trojan war—not for a woman but a bull. Now King Ailill suspects Fergus and sends his charioteer Culius to spy on him. Culius goes and not inopportunely finds Fergus in bed with Queen Maeve. He steals his sword and brings it back as a sign to Ailill.

' "There is your sign," says Culius.

'The two men looked at one another and smiled.

' "She had no choice," said Ailill. "She did it to win his help on the Tain." (This is the central expedition of the epic.) '

Fergus, his pleasures consummated, his alliance won, now buckles on his weapons and finds his scabbard empty. Excusing himself to the Queen he takes his charioteer's sword, goes into the wood . . . and cuts himself a *wooden* blade! That incident recorded bleakly, without comment has an irony as stony-faced as the Ulster hills among whose defiles these primitive amours took place. However, such incidents and dry humours are few, probably because the 'epic' is really not so much an 'epic' as the stuff of an epic awaiting its Homer who never came. It is therefore rather optimistic of Vendryes to write:—*

'I know nothing so variegated as this Irish epic material. We get the marvellous and the gross, tragedy and humour, lyricism and buffoonery. Beside superhuman figures, remnants of the mythical past, there appear human portraits sketched out of common everyday life. The Ulstermen's counsellor Sencha is a real man. So is the jocose Bricriu. The Clothru incident must, doubtless, be explained by a reference to primitive habits.' (This refers to the cohabitation of Maeve's daughter Clothru with her three brothers.) 'But the episode where Maeve shelters behind the

* Revue Celtique. XXXIX, 366: in the course of a review of Thurneysen's *Heldensage.*

shields is merely a comic invention.' (The reference is to
an incident during the wild rout of the Connaught-men
when Maeve is inconveniently seized by a necessity of nature.) 'But why is all this medley amalgamated in this saga
in the form in which we now have it? What plan had its
authors in mind? What concept of life was it that possessed
them?'

The Irish Dualism

Surely they had not arrived so far? They were content
to be excited or astonished. Synthesis could wait. All one
can feel certain of is that this strange medley of myth
and realism must have been forged by a strangely dual
mind oscillating perpetually between the wonderful and
the familiar, and more often deep in the wonderful than
adverting to the familiar: for the familiar, as I have said,
is the least frequent element and is drowned generally
in wonder.* Possibly the greatest degree of objectivity
that the native mind can have reached when listening
to these half-credible, half-incredible wonders—which, as
with the folk of to-day or yesterday, was not just something adverted to occasionally and briefly but something
impinging on them at every hour of their lives—was that
of the old West Cork woman who was recently asked,
'Do you really believe in the fairies?' and who replied,
'I do not, but they're there!' It is irrelevant for the scholars, in their preoccupation with the origins of tales, to say
that when mortals come and go, Orpheus-like, between
this world and the Otherworld—as in the beautiful love-

---

* American readers who may like to test this for themselves may consult
the translation offered by Joseph Dunn, *The Ancient Irish Epic Tale, Táin
Bó Cúalnge*. (David Nutt, London, 1914). Dunn was professor at the Catholic University, Washington. Also, *Ancient Irish Tales*, edited by Tom Peete
Cross and Clark Harris Slover (both of the University of Chicago); London,
1935.

story of Midir and Etain—we are not to take this literally because these voyagers are, of course, former deities humanised by later redactors. In humanising the gods the recreators simultaneously made their doings more wonderful, more natural, more earthy, and more monstrous. They dilated the human imagination that had to cope with the half-divine immensely more than if they had left it wholly divine.

One feels, then, from the beginning of the Christian period, in the presence of a delightful dualism—moderns would call it splitmindedness—whenever one wanders into this early Irish world. There may be an overlay of stern Christian morality. At bottom there is a joyous pagan amorality. They believe in Hell. They also believe in the Happy Isles. They believe in the Christian doctrine of punishment or compensation in the afterlife. They believe, simultaneously, in the continuance of life's normal mortal joys and sorrows for all beyond the setting sun and behind the dripping udders of the clouds. With one lobe of their minds they live what Vendryes has called the life of a

'free, independent and impetuous people, drunk on war and victory . . . (full of) the joy of adventure even in the land of fairies . . . a sense of marvel felt in the chronicles penned by the monks in the silence of the convent; for even in the holy legends and the lives of the saints one hears an echo of it, giving us a hagiography so different to that of the continent.'

Another lobe of their minds, or is it the same lobe, shot-silk at the turn of a fold, a trick of the sun, must unseat their lusty human joy, their gay reliance, leaving them hung in mid-air between their various heavens and earths.

To sum up, the Celt never formulated a religion. The very extravagance with which his imagination peopled this life with glorious, half-mortal beings tells us that though he could sublimate this world he could not transcend it. His idea of Heaven is free of Time but it is rooted in Place. He never passed out of the animistic stage of belief in what we may call devils or angels, and Christianity was therefore easily able to push aside a paganism so sparse of thought that we may say it was without thought. Imagination alone cannot formulate a religion; it can scarcely even aspire to it. Something was, perhaps is, missing in the Celt of whose presence we are at once aware in the Greeks, the Hebrews and the Oriental peoples. Was it that they had an inadequate ethical sense? Was it that they loved life too well, so that one may think, for example, that the concept of the Fall of Man, the greatest contribution made by the Jews to modern religious thought, could never have come from a people so imaginatively in love with Man himself?

The Poets' Picture

THE BEST old Irish poets are the anonymous lyrists, some Christian, mostly pagan, but all eloquent of that free and mobile life of which Vendryes speaks so affectionately. We will find the most attractive human pictures of that early Irish world, I suggest, not in the greater sagas but in these pre-tenth-century lyrics and the Middle Irish Ossianic tales and poems. Their constant motifs are the open-air, the hunt, the changing seasons, love, animals, food and drink. That life seems very close to us when, for example, Oisin, returning to earth after hundreds of years in the Land of the Young, finds his old pagan world gone and the new Hero reigning—Saint Patrick. He is listening to the saint, humbly and sadly, when, suddenly, he hears the blackbird's whistle. Lifting his hand he cries:

The call of the blackbird of Derrycairn,
The belling of the stag from Caill na gCaor,
That is the music by which Finn met early sleep;
And the wild duck of Loch na dTri Caol,

The grouse in Cruachan Cuinn,
The otter whistling in Druim da Loch,
The eagle crying in Gleann na bFuath,
The laughter of the cuckoo in Cnoc na Scoth;

The dogs barking from Gleann Caoin
The scream of the eagle from Cnoc na Sealg,
The pattering of the dogs returning early
From the Strand of the Red Stones . . .

Ah! When Finn and the Fian lived
They loved the mountain better than the monastery,
Sweet to them the blackbird's call.
They would have despised the tonguing of your bells!

We get the same intimate touch when this aged Oisin
allows his 'poor bald pate' to be washed by a Christian
woman and remembers the time when his hair was long
and fine and fair, and how his teeth, now mere sunken
rocks, 'would crunch the yellow-topped nuts.'

They'd gnaw the haunch of a stag,
Hard and hungry and hound-like;
They'd not leave a jot or a joint
That they would not mince.

Love and the chase are mingled in one of the sweetest
of all these poems—Grainne's sleep-song for her lover
Diarmuid one night when, worn out by their flight from
their enemies, he falls asleep (so one imagines it) with
his head in her lap and she, listening to the little noises
all around from the disturbed animals in the darkness,
knows their enemies must be near, but says, softly:

Sleep a little, a little little,
thou needst not feel or fear or dread,
lad to whom I give my love,
Son of O'Duibhne—Diarmuid . . .

The stag is not asleep in the east,
he never ceases belling,

although he is cosy in the blackbirds' wood,
he has no mind for sleep.

Why is not the hornless doe asleep,
calling for her speckled calf?
Running over the tops of the bushes
she cannot sleep in her lair.

The linnet is awake and twittering
above the tips of the swaying trees:
they are all chattering in the woods—
and even the thrush is not asleep.

Why does not the wild duck sleep,
not sleep, nor drowse?
Why does it not sleep in its nest?
Why is it swimming steadily with all its strength?

To-night the grouse does not sleep
above the high, stormy, heathery hill;
sweet the cry of her clear throat,
sleepless among the streams.

Caoilte, O Diarmuid, is loosed on thy track!
Caoilte's running will not take him astray.
May nor death nor dishonour touch thee—
but leave thee, rather, in an everlasting sleep . . .

It is in these lyrics that one gets the clearest vignette
in old Irish literature of that free mobile life of the fern,
before there ever was even a coastal town in Ireland.
Here pictures form clearly, come out of the abstruseness
of contemporary or local mythical references now hardly
to be understood, like little snatches of landscape through
a mountain mist; as when Deirdre, taken away from her
lover Naoisi by the lustful old King Conchubar, remem-

bers sadly the happy days when she and Naoisi and his two brothers lived in the mountains.

'Yes!' she says. 'You are proud of your soldiers marching into your palace after a foray, and think them a glorious sight. But how lovely it was to see—

Naoisi brewing the mead from the sweet hazel nuts,
Or bathing with me beside the fire,
Or Ardan with an ox or a fat hog,
Or Ainnle crossing the flooded river with faggots on his
    back.

'You think your pipers and your trumpeters make fine music? But—

It was lovely when the voice of Naoisi
Rose like a wave,
Or Ardan stringing on his harp,
Or Ainnle humming as he went into his wild hut.

They are always particularising, these lyric poets, as when one makes Deirdre recall the litany of the glens of Scotland—

Glen Laid!
I used to sleep there under the white rocks.
Fish and flesh and rich badger
Was my share in Glen Laigh.

Glen Masain!
Tall its wild garlic, white its stalks.
We slept uneasily
Over the rough estuary of Masain.

Glen Eitchi!
There I raised my first house.
Delightful its wood, after rising.
A pen for the sun was Glen Eitchi.

Glen Da Ruadh!
Welcome every man who has a right to it,
Sweet is the cuckoo on the bending branch,
On the peak above Glen Da Ruadh.

'Image after image clinches in a line some aspect of the season in their poems on winter and summer. Who will not recognise winter itself in,

A river is each furrow on the slope,

or summer in,

The sail gathers, perfect peace!

Or who needs to be told what season this is:

Blades of corn lie around corn-fields
over the region of the brown world,

or fail to feel the spring in each line of:

The cold will spring up in one's face:
the ducks of the pool have raised a cry,
from wildernesses wolf-packs scent
the early rise of morning-time.

'I have said that we know nothing about these poets, whether they were men or women, young or old—and yet I think one can tell safely that they were, whatever they professed to be, pure pagans. There is not the slightest trace of even a pantheistic belief in their Nature verse; Nature *was*, and nothing more: as in this random, and isolated, quatrain:

Cold the night in Moin Moir,
A powerful rain-storm pours down.

A wild tune—at which the clear wind laughs—
is wailing over the shelter of the woods.

One can believe that the poet turned with an equal vital-
ity to almost everything that in his daily life he had to
meet. That objectivity recompenses us for the mystery
of his name. If we but let a little freedom to our sympathies we can feel back at his side in an instant, unsun-
dered by strangeness in his beliefs or ours, at one with his
delight, indifferent to his mask.

'When he says, with the air of a man looking over a half-
door, in another isolated scrap:

> A little bird
> Has let a piping from the tip
> Of his shining yellow beak—
> The blackbird from the yellow-leaved tree
> Has flung his whistle over Loch Laig.

(and that, by the way, is all there is of it) we can surely
feel the same physical delight, the same identical pleasure
that he felt, and nothing to mar that pleasure but the
withdrawal of our smile in thinking, with a melancholy
that has nothing to do with the little poem, that bird, and
tree, and whistle—and man—passed out of this world almost a thousand years ago.' *

The synthesis, there, is a personal one; the achievement
is individual; and this will not be the only place in which
the heart-beat of genius seems to be the best interpreter
of the race.

---

* This quotation and the translations are from my anthology of old Irish
poetry, *The Silver Branch* (The Viking Press). Far better translations,
though less literal, occur in Frank O'Connor's *Fountain of Magic*. The best
translations of all, literal, scholarly, sensitive, are in Kuno Meyer's *Ancient
Irish Poetry*.

The Social Reality

THE WAY of life that lies behind these lyrics and those romances was at once pastoral and warlike; that of a people who varied their modest agriculture and the tending of their vast herds by border wars to add to their wealth. They lived free, casual lives under the open sky inside (and the adjective is paramount) *local* horizons; which means that they remained, in dwindling enclaves of antiquity, up to the seventeenth century and the completion of the English conquest, a regionalist people who never developed a commercial sense, an elaborate husbandry, or a town-life. The Danes and the Normans founded every Irish town that exists; the Tudors founded the rest. Dublin, Wexford, Wicklow, Limerick, Cork—all Danish. Kilkenny is a typical Norman creation. The Irish never founded a town. The finest thing they did in this way was the creation of monastic settlements, and these time scattered as the wind blows the ash of a burnt-out fire.

No towns, then, unlike Roman Britain; no roads; only beaten paths, stony or muddy; very few buildings, an enclosed, possibly covered-over rath or earthen circle, bothies of clay and woven branches—for architecture, as we know it, comes only with Christianity in small, but often very graceful churches of the type called Hiberno-Romanesque; everywhere dark and wellnigh impassable woods—battles in 'passes' that generally meant passes through forests; a climate even more moist than in our time; vast stretches of uninhabited land; and everywhere the country's gold—herds of cattle; a great chieftain or 'king' would own a hundred thousand cows. One may imagine how it was that the Danes could never penetrate far beyond the coast, except for brief and daring raids inland, and that even the Normans could only drive wedges into the more passable valleys, and then always have inimical and unconquerable fastnesses on their flanks. One might also hazard that the life-mode of such a land could defy the challenges of the outer world a very long time: it actually persisted with an amazing toughness until the seventeenth century, so that in the heyday of Queen Elizabeth great parts of Ireland were still living much as their ancestors had lived in the days of Cuchulainn.

'The leit-motif of Gaelic society from time immemorial had been the lowing of cattle. So persistent and dominant was that note in the lives of the generations, raised almost to the stature of a myth by the national epic, *The Tain Bo Cuailgne* (*The Driving of the Bull of Cooley*), that the Bull might well have become the Bull God and some ingenious scholar may yet interpret the Dagda not as the Good Father, the Sun, but as the All Father, the Bull, to be adored as an emblem of fertility, a guarantee of a life that need never languish. About these beasts centred raid and counter-raid, the ambitions of kings and queens, great battles, scandalous loves, the tremendous exploits of the sagas.' In a sentence, Ireland's wealth was for centuries in its soft rains, its vast pasturages, those wandering herds. About this simple commerce there developed a life-mode that was at once dangerous and secure, unconcerned and anxious, reckless and rapacious, unambitious and adventurous, as peaceful and yet as bloody as the desert.

The Family Groups

One has to appreciate that there were no 'clans' in Ireland. The core of the acknowledged order was the family, but the lock-knit family system did not develop. The limits of the sacred nexus were symbolised by the hand. The palm was the common ancestor; the joints of the fingers were his descendants unto his grandchildren; the finger-nails were his great-grandchildren. The family was not supposed to exist beyond that.

The chieftainship of these family-groups was a hereditary gift qualified by public election, and the society of which they were the nucleus was finely graded. There was not much that was democratic about it. Tradition and practice held firmly to a structure ranging slowly downward from king to slave. But it contained one satisfactory element. That 'true family-group' which has been described, known as the *deirbh-fine* (pronounced derv-finneh) lived together—early marriages made this possible—and they shared property in common, grandfather and grandchildren alike, and their hold on their land was absolute and incontestable. No chief, or king, had any claim on any land other than his own. He could not legally dispossess any family in his small kingdom, which gave the families a considerable liberty of action, at any rate in theory. He could, of course, conquer and dispossess as many families outside his kingdom as he was able to snatch from a neighbouring king; he could raid and take the lands on his border; he might take neighbouring chieftains as his lieges, and the more ambitious and able

any chief of families was the nearer he approached the
rank and fame of those kings whom history has preserved
by name, until, if he were a really powerful man, he
might alter the shape of history itself, like that Brian
Boru who became king of all Ireland and defeated Danish ambitions, or that Dermot MacMurrough who, to
serve his private ambitions, brought in the Normans.

Upper-class Life

From literature and history we form some idea of the
lives of those 'upper classes.' The sagas glorify their lives
and persons, cluster them with a jewelled magnificence
through which it is difficult to visualise the reality. Thus
in the tale called *The Wooing of Emer* we read a description of King Conchobar's house, the Red Branch, which
goes as follows:

'Nine compartments were in it from the fire to the wall.
Thirty feet was the height of each *bronze partition* of the
house. *Carvings* of red yew therein. A wooden floor beneath
and *roofings of tiles* above. The compartment of Conchobar was in the front of the house, with a *ceiling of silver,*
with *pillars of bronze.* Their *head-pieces glittered with gold*
and were *set with carbuncles* so that day and night were
equally light therein. There was a *gong of silver* above the
king, hung from the roof-tree of the royal house. Whenever
Conchobar struck the gong with his royal rod all the men
of Ulster were silent. The twelve cubicles of the twelve
chariot-chiefs were around about the king's compartment.
All the valiant warriors of the men of Ulster found space in
that king's house at the time of drinking and yet no man
of them could crowd the other. In it were held great and
numerous gatherings of every kind and wonderful pastimes.
Games and music and singing there, heroes performing

their feats, poets singing, harpers and players on the tim-
pan striking up their sounds.'

Such descriptions, if they may be so called, are obviously
idealised and conventional. Not that beautiful ornaments
do not remain to show us that there is a substratum of
truth in these colourful pictures. But when I ask the
scholars what examples we actually possess of those items
that I have put into italics I am told that we have none.
For the reality one has to picture a less decorative existence: the largest structures were single-room barn-like
buildings, with bunks or couches, in the middle a fire
and its utensils, the smoke vacillating to a vent in the roof,
the main ventilation through the doorways which would
be closed in wild weather by pads of woven wattle, and
all protected outside by one or more earthen moats—those
circular raths of which many are to be seen to-day, all
covered now with briars and brambles, preserved largely
by the superstition of later ages which called them fairy-
raths and feared to disturb them. Not that these *duns,* or
raths, would have been without civility. They would often
be lime-white as snow, 'as if,' says one tale about one such
rath, 'all the lime in Ireland had been used on it'; they
would have had their simple wines; and beers in vats of
red yew; and their valuable hunting hounds so prized that
a poem could be written on the death of a loved dog, and
we can well believe that the hero Fionn slept beside his
hound Conbeg. Even the women might have their pet-
dogs; though we know little of the life of woman in those
centuries beyond fleeting glimpses, as when we hear of
Credhe painting her eyebrows with the juice of berries;
or of the love-charms of the women of the Fianna ('who
washed in a bath made of those herbs and so compelled

their husbands to their love') ; or of Fionn's 'she-runner,'
or as we would now say dispatch-rider; and occasionally
we hear of amazons fighting beside their men. Indeed it
is probable that the undecorated reality of that half-bar-
baric life would, if we could but know it, be far more
interesting than the romanticised version of the poets.
Curiously we do not hear of the women hunting with the
men though the descriptions of the hunts which would
have gone out from and come back to these *duns* are many
and vivid. At random I choose this typical little hunting
picture, which happens to come at the close of the day's
chase, and is lighted only by the stars: *

'Thence they proceeded to Coill na mBuidhen or The
Wood of the Companies, now called Coill Muadnatan, or
Muadnait's wood, and over the brow of Gulban Gort, or
Ben Gulban and to Grabh Ros or the Deerherds Grove.
There they make a capacious booth for cooking. They
roof it in with sedge, green in the top, pale towards the
roots, and they secure it with ties over all, and there they
begin the branding and seething of their flesh. Says a man
of them:—
    ' "Is there water near us?"
'Caoilte answered, "Surely there is Ossian's well."
    ' "It is a dark night," said the others.
    ' "Not to me is it dark," said Caoilte, "for in Ireland's
five great provinces there is not a spot in which, whether
out of rock or out of river, a cuachful is procured both by
day and night but I am at home there."
    'In his one hand therefore he took a silver cup, in the
other his thickshafted solid-socketed spears, and walked
straight to a well. He heard a sound of water being troubled
and what should be there but a long-flitched boar that
drank. Into the riveted, well-poised spear's thong he put
his finger and delivered a cast which killed the swine.

* From *Silva Gadelica*, II. The Colloquy with the Ancients. Translated
by Standish Hayes O'Grady. (London, 1892.)

'Then with his full cup of water still in his hand he brought him away upon his back.'

This Caoilte is later, in his old age, pictured as remembering such nights as that for the benefit of Saint Patrick, and as he recalls them he 'wept tearfully in sadness so that his very breast was wet.' To make a leap forward in time, I think we may accept it that this is not merely a pretty poetic note but a true reflection of something set deeply and permanently in the Irish nature. The love of sport and the active life of the open-air is too persistent, in every century, to be denied, so that the difference of temper between the Fenian romances and the romances of Charles Lever is, in this regard, imperceptible. It may be noted, too, that those Fenian tales were still being told over the fires in the cabins in Lever's day. The old and the young men who heard them would not, the following morning, on hearing the baying of the hounds and the 'He's away!' feel any disjunction of mood or excitement as they ran to the nearest ditch and saw those modern Caoiltes (now of the Fifteenth Enniskillens) streaming in their red coats across the uplands. To these latest usurpers of the lordship of Irish sport the 19th century watchers on the ditch would have given the same envy, the same admiration that, in Caoilte's day, the serfs or *daoscarsluagh,* as they are called in Gaelic, gave to their native sportsmen, their native lords. Sport, in Ireland, is the nearest thing to an inviolable enclave that we know, resisting to the last ditch the intrusion of prejudices that disrupt every other common ground, holding at bay the fervours of nationalism and even of religion itself. The glorification of the sporty Anglo-Irishman with which we are familiar in literature could not have occurred without the connivance of the native Irish peasant. He had to have a hero, and if it were not Caoilte or Red Hugh O'Donnell, then the bucks of the Big House had to do instead.

500 A.D. *to* 1600 A.D.

We must return to *circa* A.D. 500. Time altered the life-mode of Ireland so very slowly that descriptions by six-teenth-century travellers are probably fairly valid for the fifth century. They all agree on the simplicity of Irish life as it appeared to them, much of it spent in the open air. When the Sir John Harington who translated *Orlando Furioso* visited the great Hugh O'Neill in Ulster in 1599, a cultured and travelled Irish prince who had been reared in the household of Sir Philip Sidney's father, he was en-tertained by O'Neill to a meal and conversation beside fern tables, on fern forms, spread under the canopy of heaven. O'Neill's children were in velvet and gold-lace; his bodyguard of beardless boys were stripped to the waist. Other travellers make us see how the smoke in the houses still wanders indecisively to the vent; the milk strained through straw; the great candle that gutters and smells. The most part of the people dress in the famous Irish mantle, furhooded, triangular, with little underneath but a kilted shirt. Others have their long-sleeved saffron shirts of linen, breeches, shoes of skins. And some of these ob-servers find it all 'heathenish and savage,' and some record it with a sober and respectful interest, knowing that it is an ancient and complex society, powerful, wealthy, hon-ourable, creative in its own manner, dangerous to under-estimate. Had these sixteenth-century travellers been transported back to pre-Christian times their comments would probably have been more respectful, but their pic-tures would not have been greatly different. Dürer's picture of Irish soldiers would probably scarcely need to be altered to depict the age of the great pagan sagas. At no time, however, do we form any intimate picture of the life of the lower grades, largely because both letters and society were graded upwards to a caste, and both 'bards' and 'chiefs' had the aristocratic outlook. Thus, in recording the casualties at the Battle of Mag Tured, the historian opens by saying—'I know not the number of peasants and rabble,' and goes at once to the 'lords and nobles and kings' sons and overkings'; ending with—'we reckon only a few of the servants of the overkings.' These horsemen, kernes (later, employed soldiers) were at the bottom rung of freemen: below them came the helots—men without a vote, men without a craft and even the inferior craftsmen, the common labourer, strangers in a district. None of these have any place in the barbarically splendid literature of the sagas, except, perhaps, as 'rabble' or as 'buffoons.' Not until the sixteenth century does anybody much care what happens to them and then it was not the Irish chiefs but the English chiefs who speak of them, in some pity and consideration.

A Brittle Bond

The system as a whole, then, is not feudal. But both in practice and in time the distinction balances on a knife-edge. For ambitious dynasts, whose doings form such a tedious greater part of Irish history, swarmed. In theory chiefs and kings were elected. Since, in fact, they held power partly by an atavistic loyalty to 'the ould stock,' and partly by proving their worth as fighting-men and buccaneers, they depended on their lieges, or clients, and their lieges depended on them. These lieges, or clients were not in theory feudal vassals. They might say, or boast that they could say: 'My chief's ambitions are no concern of mine.' But in their hearts they knew quite well that the ambitions of some neighbouring king were definitely a great concern of theirs. And to which concern should they, at any given moment, pay the greater attention? That was always the question that affected their loyalties. Intermarriage and patronage created a royal nexus that cemented them to their traditional leader by every human bond of blood, affection, tradition, and self-interest. It worked in times of peace. Militarily (and politically) the bond was fragile. One visualises a brittle society. In fact a large-scale border-war would crack it wide open.

Thus, though Vendryes speaks of 'a free, independent and impetuous people, drunk on war and victory' he does not fail to see, also, that a price had to be paid for that: the price was that this life should be not only free but fractional, not only intimate but too individualist and haughty to melt into a national unity and a national organisation. In three words it was aristocratic, regional and personal, and all three to an extreme degree.

Regionalism Not Unity

It is well to insist that this indifference to political unity is a very different matter to the Celts' powerful, racial, linguistic, and sentimental sense of oneness. For they seem to have had no difficulty in combining this strong sense of their racial oneness with an equally strong insistence on their regional otherness; which ultimately seems to have nourished the fatal delusion that to flourish as a people it was not necessary to formulate the political concept of the nation.

In practice, as a result, a very small island was divided into five parts, called *cuigi* (the same word still means 'province' in modern Gaelic) ; and these fifths were further subdivided into small, fluid regions called *tuatha*. The number of people in modern Ireland who might claim to be descended from ancient kings is therefore large because the number of ancient kings was numberless. There was no central organisation. One reads of High Kings, and there were strong men, like the famous Brian Boru, who by sheer force dominated the whole island for brief periods, but the essential factor is that there was no legal position whatsoever known as *the* Irish king.

In fact no recognised legal system (corresponding to any modern legal system) existed at all. The so-called Brehon Laws—the written laws as we have them in the manuscripts—were not a code which grew up piecemeal over centuries of disagreement and ultimate agreement, like modern case-law, nor a system developed by legislation. They were, quite simply, a highly idealised picture, composed 'in the study,' of what popular practices and habits and traditions would be like (or might be like) in terms of law if legalists were asked by some dictator to codify these habits, practices and traditions and he could apply sanctions to enforce them. The Brehon Laws in other words, as we know them, emanate from legal schools, not from any central authority. Many of them seem to be unfeasible. In so far as they depict actual practices the evidence seems to be that these practices varied widely according to regions.

A Primitive Society

Our picture, then, admittedly sketched in the barest outline like a simple map or cartoon, is of an intimate, local society, very elastic, fluid, and free, admirable and even enviable so long as neighbours did not too bloodily spoil one another, or some more efficient organisation did not challenge it from outside. It has been called primitive and the term has been resented, and, up to a point (in time) I think rightly resented, for it not merely worked but it was under it—as we shall see—that Ireland made her greatest contribution to the civilisation of Europe and had one of her own most creative periods in the arts. This is a fact that historians who judge these chronic nonconformists by the standards of Roman or Norman discipline must not ignore.

Those imperial-minded peoples fulfilled their genius magnificently through a corporate technique of living; these Irish also splendidly fulfilled their genius through a technique of dispersion and disconnection—up to the eleventh century, during which long stretch of time everything they produced was superior to the products of most of their contemporaries. But, after that date, the word 'primitive' becomes irrefutable, when the development of most other European countries, in science, the arts, the amenities of life, all the techniques of peace and war began to leave the less organised countries behind in the race.

The patriotic Irish view of the conquest of Ireland by colonising Britain is that her civilisation was finally destroyed by a more efficient and ruthless military organisation. Perhaps it would be more correct to say that the consolidated Tudor state was too strong an opponent for Irish regionalism. But, if we take the longest view of history, there was more to it even than that. The Danes and the Normans had prepared the way, and three things that they brought were mortal—ports, roads, towns. From these everything followed. As well might the free-riding Arabs of the desert have smelled disaster on seeing the first merchants settle on their coast as the Irish seeing the first little Danish settlements twinkle at night on the edge of the sea, and know that this deviltry was not just something to be scorned from the hilltop and the fern, but something that they had to come to terms with. The Irish were too arrogant and too freedom-loving to come to terms with the 'hucksters' ' life. When it was too late they fought, with tremendous dash and deathless courage, but, as the system dictated, it was each man for his own horizon, and they were destroyed piecemeal.

Irish Individualism

To sum up, there lay in the Irish mind, and still may lie, atavistically indestructible, an ineradicable love of individual liberty. Equality, so far as I can see, they never bothered about. They clung to the family unit because there was a good deal of individual liberty inside it. Roman Law, which was to come in with the Normans, had another idea—or had by the time the Irish met it. For in early Roman law the family system was also sacred—see the inferior position of woman, for example, subject even in her widowhood to agnates in order that the family structure might be kept intact; but as the idea of the Roman State developed the intimate idea of the Family began to yield ground to the larger concept of

Society. This idea never appealed to the Irish. True, the Roman State stepped in with donations of individual rights—to women for example—but when individual rights are bestowed by the State the gift is double-edged. It may be an improvement to go from domestic despotism to state paternalism; but it is, undeniably, easier to fight one's own battle with one's father than to fight it with some remote 'father,' and it is, so to speak, more fun. In the Italian communes the old Germanic idea and the Roman idea were conjoined for hundreds of years in just the same uneasy way. And for the same reason, that the Germans brought with them from their forests that greater personal independence which always belongs to small groups, it took a long time for the Longobardic system to blend with the Roman in the great mediaeval and Renaissance republics.

In modern Eire a good deal of lip-service is paid to the family-unit. If there is, in this, any backward glance at the old Celtic system it is wholly sentimental. In practice we owe all the *legal* rights and restrictions that we enjoy and accept to the 'brutal' Normans and the 'brutal' Tudors who are supposed to be equally responsible for the 'seven hundred years of slavery' about which our patriots often glibly talk without knowing anything much about it. If the Celtic tradition has given us anything in this field, what it has given is an atavistic individualism which tends to make all Irishmen inclined to respect no laws at all; and though that may be socially deplorable it is so humanly admirable, and makes life so much more tolerable and charitable and easy-going and entertaining, that one hopes that it is, in fact, something for which one may praise and bless 'the good ould days.'

II · THE TRUNK

Political History

c. 600-1100	*Monasticism develops. Missionaries flock to the Continent.*
c. 800	*Danish invasions begin. First coastal towns and ports.*
1014	*Battle of Clontarf checks Danish power.*
1169-	*The Normans. Many inland towns and roads. Urbanisation begins. Celtic heyday over.*
1200-1500	*Norman assimilation. Urbanisation develops and affects the Irish life-mode. Modern sophistication begins. This period is politically blank.*
c. 1521-	*Tudor pressure begins. Reformation doctrines introduced and resisted.*

Asceticism and Classicism

WHEN the traveller to-day comes on tiny, ruined Roman-esque churches in such lonely places as Glendalough, in the Wicklow mountains, or Clonmacnoise on the Shan-non, or on desolate islands about the coast, he may know that here lived either an ascetic or a student, and that here he is touching on ground that was for a long period a battle-ground of the Irish mind.

Latin Christianity gave the Irish their first international challenge and opportunity: they took both eagerly. The first contemporary reference to an Irishman who was also a Christian is characteristically dramatic. It is a furious reference in the letters of Saint Jerome (415-16) to 'an ignorant caluminator . . . full of Irish porridge' who has had the insolence to criticise him. This man was the heresiarch Pelagius, founder of Pelagianism, a man of great intellectual power. He defended himself in Jerusa-lem against Orosius, who had to employ an interpreter. He was in Rome before Alaric sacked it—we are now mov-ing forward to the decay of the Roman world and stand at the brink of the Dark Ages. There Pelagius wrote his *Commentaries on the Epistles of Saint Paul.* He went on to Africa, and so on to Asia. In Jerusalem he vanishes from history. He is the great antagonist of the stern teach-ings of Saint Augustine on freewill and grace. He pro-claimed the freedom of the personality and man's power to make his own soul unaided. His doctrine has persisted, in one form or another, down to the days of Jansenism and Pascal. It was to counter his teachings that the first Saint Patrick—there were, as we now know, two Saint Patricks —caused Germanus of Auxerre to be sent to Britain and himself, later, to Ireland. His heretical views were highly untypical; otherwise he is but one of hundreds, if not of thousands, who from the fifth to the ninth century carried into Europe not only the teachings of Christianity but a learning greater than Europe then possessed.

A Great Heretic

At the other end of this great period of efflorescence was an even more striking example, perhaps the greatest individual figure that the Irish presented to mediaeval Europe, John Eriugena (Irish-born John), also to be counted heretical. He spoke Greek and Latin. He was a philosopher of considerable charm, a daring and original thinker, of whom it has been said that

'while his contemporaries were only lisping in philosophy, and even his successors for centuries did no more than discuss a small number of disconnected questions, Eriugena in the ninth century worked out a complete philosophical synthesis. Apart from those incredibly daring speculations which made him the *enfant terrible* of his time he reads like a pantheistic contemporary of Saint Thomas.' *

His knowledge of neo-Platonist philosophy was so intimate, indeed unique in northern Europe, that he was

* I am guided throughout this section mainly by Kenney's *Sources for the Early History of Ireland*. Vol. 1. (New York, 1929.) The quotation is from De Wulf, *History of Mediaeval Philosophy* (1909, p. 167).

the only man whom Charles the Bald could find to translate a Christian neo-Platonist manuscript sent to him from
Constantinople as a present from the Emperor.

These two men offer us an extraordinary picture of a
remote island, hitherto counted as barbarian, suddenly
flowering into civilisation, taking back to Europe riches
that might otherwise have remained buried for centuries
under the ruins of the Empire. The great paleographer
Traube puts the general statement in its most extreme
form: 'Whoever on the continent in the days of Charles
the Bald knew Greek was an Irishman, or at least his
knowledge was transmitted to him through an Irishman,
or the report which endows him with this glory is false.'

A Great 'Enthusiast'

A third man reveals a very different spirit to John
Eriugena, a strain of what we might nowadays call the
'Puritanism' of the Irish mind—a strain which nothing
in the romances or the lyrics foreshadow. This man is
Columbanus, the great apostle of Irish asceticism, to
become well-known abroad for his stern Monastic Rule.
This counsellor of self-mortification and penance—an
ideal which was to run wild among the Irish cenobites—
founded at Luxeuil a religious colony which was one of
the germinal centres of European monasticism.

And yet, although this asceticism is a disturbing and
puzzling contrast with the humanism of Pelagius and the
charm of Eriugena and the sweetness of many delicate
notes cast elsewhere (though not typically) through the
literature of the Irish Church, its founder also loved the
old classical learning, read—at any rate read in—Virgil

and Horace, Ovid and Juvenal, may have read some of
Persius and Lucan; and wrote Latin verse which has
been considered remarkable for language, style and ver-
satility. One might, making large allowances for a personal strictness, be tempted to see here another synthesis
—an intelligent Christian synthesis—if he were not the
leader of a wholesale flight to an extreme: if one did not
know that around this cenobitic life which he established
there grew up another vast literature whose extravagances
suggest that this is but another wild oscillation in a racial
mind still insufficiently experienced or trained to be able
to cope with the new, Christian wonder.

'The mind of the Irish people,' says Kenney,

'during the early Christian era was, fundamentally, the
product of countless ages of paganism. The popular legends
(of saints and hermits) , moulded under a pagan or semi-
pagan attitude of mind, contained a large amalgam of
"magic" and "superstition," those survivals of primitive
religion. So far, therefore, as the *acta sanctorum* depend
on popular legend they are, in some degree, records of
primitive religious ideas and practices. Irish paganism
seems to have consisted of a lower *stratum,* deep and wide,
of magical belief and practice, and, superimposed thereon,
an upper section of mythology. Myth and magic were
ejected from their positions of supremacy by the coming
of Christianity, but the evidence does not indicate that the
sphere of operation of either was extensively diminished.' *

And he points to the curious fact that it is in the later
mediaeval texts that this pagan survival is most marked;
as if Christianity, in becoming more and more widely
accepted, became debased accordingly.

* *Op. cit.,* p. 302. On the saint as the new 'medicine-man.'

Two Notes Clashing

Christianity thus restates the internal imaginative and political struggle in an intellectual form. Where that little ruined church is alone and remote one may guess at a saintly cenobite and at magic fables; where a round tower's gray finger points to the sky one may presume a larger settlement and streets of bothies nestling under the stone remains, and one is likely to come on traditions of a famous school of learning. How can the two notes be harmonised?

Here one must pause to note another immense problem in that characteristic regionalism at which we have glanced in the section called 'The Social Reality.' For when monasticism became the regular Irish church system the effect was against episcopal or diocesan organisation and for rule by local abbots, chosen (as in the secular society of the *deirbh-fine* or true family) from blood-relations of the founder, with the inevitable local autonomy, sometimes, even in religious matters, established by bonds of blood between the regional 'state' and the regional monastery and its regional offshoots. That abuses would arise out of this lack of centralisation was natural. For example, to give but one, the heirship (called the *co-arb*ship) of Saint Patrick at Armagh had, by the twelfth century, passed by hereditary succession for fifteen generations, and in eight cases had been filled by married laymen.

Perhaps, however, the deeper truth here is not so much concerned with Irish monasticism as with monasticism as a system anywhere, though the dangers were aggravated in Ireland by peculiar local conditions. The virtues inherent in monastic systems, that is to say, require autonomy in order to flourish. The monk is the leaven not the loaf. But the orders have always had their heyday and their dogday, and whereas in their heyday they may be given full rein it is necessary in their decline to merge them back quickly into the general discipline of Christendom. Meanwhile it is above all necessary that a strong parent church should keep a careful watch lest these outliers should be exploited by the secular forces about them. In Ireland there was no organised parent church to do this. The old Irish passion for blood and place, and other passions as well, ran riot until the Norman reformation established central church government.

The New Heroes

Why did the Irish seize so wholeheartedly on Columbanian monasticism? To quote Kenney again—

'The decisive reason for the dominance of monasticism in Ireland was, we may be sure, the enthusiasm with which the early Irish Christians embraced the coenobitical life and the ideals of asceticism; this it was that provided inmates, sometimes in their thousands, for all the monasteries and, as the spirit of asceticism grew, sent Irish anchorites to seek hermitages on the islands of the Irish and Scottish coasts or overseas in foreign lands.' *

From the sixth to the twelfth century the exploits of these new heroes were heroic to the point of extravagance, a medley of more or less pointless peregrinations and penances, often repulsive, at any rate to modern minds; of prolonged pilgrimages; of true evangelisation; of valuable secular teaching. Irishmen wandered to the East, to Ice-

* Kenney, *op. cit.*, p. 293.

land, to their own most stormtorn islands, for no reason but Abraham's urge to self-banishment in God's name. *Egredere de terra tua et de cognatione tua.* Kenney, illustrating how this sacrifice of their dearest associations seems to have appealed in a peculiar manner to the Irish, aptly quotes this entry in the *Anglo-Saxon Chronicle:*

'Three Irishmen came to King Alfred in a boat without any oars, from Ireland, whence they had stolen away because they desired, for the love of God, to be in a state of pilgrimage—they recked not where.'

One must not be tempted by the bizarre tales of the extreme *penitentes* into giving them too much of the picture. The legends about them are, of course, unreliable as to detail but their popularity must suggest that they offered at least one ideal. Thus one of them is supposed to have condemned himself never to scratch; another is said to have hung from hooks under his armpits for seven years (the usual magical number) ; of another it is said that 'he used to lie the first night in the same grave with every corpse brought to his church'; another is said to have sat for the usual seven years on the backbone of a whale. And so on. The ascetic practice known as *virgines subintroductae* seems to be authentic—the habit of bringing beautiful girls into the cell of a saintly aspirant in order to give him the glory of overcoming the agonies of lust. Saint Ita was said to have kept a stagbeetle 'as big as a lapdog a-sucking her until it ate away one of her sides.'

One may here conveniently point the contrast. For there is also a delicate lyric describing how Jesukin came one night to Ita's cell, in a vision, to be nursed at her breast.

I cannot help quoting a few lines from Robin Flower's charming poem on this legend, beginning:

He came to me
A little before morning through the night
And lay between my breasts until daylight.

How helplessly
Lay the small limbs, the fallen head of gold
The little hands that clasped and could not hold. . . .

Ending,

And thence he drew
With soft stirred lips and clutching hands that strove
Sweet mortal milk and more than mortal love.

Or, again, there is the contrast of the gaiety and light-heartedness of the poem which may be called 'The Heavenly Banquet,' ascribed to Saint Bridget (who, incidentally, is held by such scholars as O'Rathaille to be the euhemerisation of a pagan goddess) :

I would like to have the men of Heaven
In my own house
With vats of good cheer
Laid out before them.

I would like to have the three Marys
Their fame is so great.
I would like to have people
From every corner of heaven.

I would like them to be cheerful
In their drinking.
I would like to have Jesus, too,
Here amongst them.

I would like to have a great lake of beer
For the King of Kings.
I'd love to be watching the family of heaven
Drinking it through all eternity.

If it has to be noted that these happy notes are, alas, comparatively few; that they represent not so much a new classical culture or a purely native culture as a Hiberno-Latin culture which never came to full bloom, they are, nevertheless, another abortive effort at a synthesis to which the pure ascetic contributed little. They are the people who (like Columbanus, unusual ascetic that he was) could bring to Europe not merely Rules and Penances but texts and learning—mainly the old Latin and Vulgate texts of the Bible, some pure, some corrupt or conflated, the works of the Fathers, geographies, histories, texts in Greek and Latin. And this dissemination of learning was most frequent after the ninth century when the Viking raids scattered the schools and the typical pilgrim Irishman then became the wandering scholar rather than the saint. Thousands of these men have disappeared into the darkness, but there is a lengthy list of important continental foundations due to them, from Fiacra—an early wanderer, he died in 670—whose hermit's cell became the monastery of Breuil (for some odd reason his name is commemorated in the French word *fiacre,* a cab), to the Marianus who built at Ratisbon, in 1076, the monastery of Saint Peter, known as the Weih-Sankt-Peter; or those others who founded monasteries so far afield as Wurzeburg, Nüremberg, Constance and Vienna. One exile went as far as Russia and came back with a load of furs whose sale completed the building of Saint James' at Ratisbon.

Asceticism Versus Classicism

One does not wish to propose a bald and obvious antinomy between asceticism and learning. Doubtless they were often mingled in the same man—I have twice mentioned the clear example of Columbanus. But one cannot deny that a struggle was going on through all those centuries between a sane discipline (under Christian and Classical influence) and a hardly sane 'discipline' (under the old pagan influence). One might even call it a struggle between the new foreign classicism and the old native romanticism. What is at stake all the time is a definition of order. That they could mingle lastingly was hardly possible. Asceticism restricts, Classicism perfects. Both attempt to order. But the one order is barren and the other is creative. Above all the one is particular and the other is general, and there is hardly any urge in this mediaeval Irish art or thought towards the general. (Even the jurists show no art of generalisation; for whenever asked a general question, such as 'What is Justice?' they will reply with the particular, 'It is Justice when so-and-so happens.') This problem of order, of form, is posed for us most interestingly by the illuminated manuscripts, such as the famous Book of Kells, each example so intricate, so devotedly pursued—one can hardly say constructed—in its own personal waywardness, so magnificent, delicate, lovely, convoluted, spontaneous, so circuitous and unpredictable that it might be taken as an image of the individualistic Irish genius at its most colourful and most tantalising. Is it fruitful, however, to reject symmetry, never to balance space evenly against space, to prefer spontaneity without pattern? Does such an art offer channels for a general development? It is certainly at a pole from the classical mode which never did fructify in Ireland—not until it returned to us in the oratory, literature, and ordered architecture of the Anglo-Irish eighteenth century.

The Monastic Failure

If these are imponderable questions there is nothing imponderable about the failure of monasticism as a religious system. It was so complete that the first real Norman invasion of Ireland was a movement of necessary church reform directed from Canterbury. By then (eleventh century) the Cluniac reform had already applied elsewhere its well-known ideals of organisation, uniformity and discipline. Archbishop Lanfranc now directed it towards Ireland. The reformers were familiar enough with continental irregularities but they were particularly shocked by conditions here. The main evil, as I have already intimated, was, as indeed it had been elsewhere, the secular intrusion. In a great many foundations the abbot had by the eleventh century become a lay lord, the monks his tenants, the students mere labourers and the priests hired servants. The Norman observers speak, too, of lax morality*—monks and priests marrying, the laity living loose lives, but this is debatable and the animadversions of Lanfranc and Saint Bernard may have arisen, at least in part, from unfamiliarity with traditional Irish marriage customs.† Church discipline was undoubtedly lax. There were, it is true, some bishops in Ireland, but it is a measure of their helplessness that there was no archbishop and no primate.

Lanfranc asserted his supremacy over the Irish and encouraged native reformers to establish an episcopal system. The Hiberno-Danish sees in the coastal towns of Dublin, Wexford, Waterford and Limerick eagerly agreed and sent their priests to Canterbury to be consecrated. Others,

* See Kenney, *op. cit.*, p. 745 foll.
† See Orpen, *Ireland under the Normans*, Vol. 1, 124. On the position of women.

equally anxious to regularise their position in the universal church, set up chapters, cathedral centres, provinces, and new monasteries under foreign monks. The corporate system thus enters, for the time effectively, on the regional Irish scene not through politics but through religion and invasion, and is one of the greatest of the Normans' gifts.

The Norman Gift

IN THE patriotic iconography of nineteenth-century Ireland the constant motifs were the round-tower, the Celtic cross, the wolfhound, the harp, and the ruined abbey. All but the abbey belong to the long period we have just closed. The abbey is Norman. But, for some reason, connected, no doubt, with the idea that the 'enslavement' of Ireland began when Dermot MacMurrough, King of Leinster, brought in the foreigner, i.e. the Normans, another one of the commonest features of the Irish landscape is generally omitted—the ruined Norman castle or keep. One sees these wrecks of time, from the train and from the road, all over the country but most commonly in the east and south, ivy-covered, perhaps no more than a broken tooth of masonry, a shelter for cattle on wet days, or a monument carefully preserved by the Board of Works. If this book were a political history we would have to deal under this head with the theme of 'seven-hundred-years-of-slavery,' i.e. beginning with those Norman conquerors' castles. Since this is a journey in the track of a mind, and our only interest is the immense gifts the Normans have brought to that amalgam of many strains which is modern Ireland, to us the Norman castle is a relic of a great civilisation.

The Norman invasion was, to begin, the gamble of a

small group of adventurers: later on the invasion became, under Henry II and his successors, a national colonisation or conquest—which was, however, never completed. The first cluster that landed at Bannow Bay, in Wexford, on May 1st 1169, consisted of thirty knights, sixty other horsemen, and about three hundred archers on foot. Within nine months they and their Irish allies had taken the walled town of Wexford from the Ostmen, subdued Dublin, and made themselves virtual masters of all Leinster. The overt reason for their success was twofold: the lack of an effective Irish centre to organise opposition—or, though we Irish do not much care for the bitter word, true that it is, Irish disunity; the second reason was superior Norman military technique. The basic Irish failure, however, was in the stubborn conservatism of their lives. They could not realise what was happening. When one king after another made his obeisances to Henry they thought that it 'meant no more than the similar acknowledgment which they had often given, and broken, to an ard-ri (or High King) . Nay, as Henry would be far off across the seas, they probably expected it to mean a great deal less.'* They had been for so long accustomed to giving hostages, often their own sons, if needs be sacrificing them to death or to blinding when agreements had to be broken, that they thought that the same feckless technique would work with these strangers. It proved to be a very different matter when these practised mail-clad knights set up those stone castles, created towns, held what towns there were (whenever the Irish, who had a claustrophobic horror of towns, took one, right up to the seventeenth century, they burned or abandoned it) , and from these centres enforced their bonds.

* Orpen, *op. cit.*, I, 284.

Towns Begin

This widespread sprouting of towns* was the most significant new thing in Irish life and the most fruitful thing the Normans ever did. They began civic life in Ireland. With roads and ports trade followed. Abbeys they established in numbers. The result was a new urbanity, a new and more elaborate life-mode, new skills, a new sweetness. For this the old Celtic world paid in blood and havoc and unrest. The little chieftains were slaughtered and robbed; 'the more important chieftains submitted to terms, accepted portions of their former territories and continued to rule there according to Irish law.' At least one is known to have become a feudal lord, indistinguishable from his Norman neighbours; and there may have been more like him. Many interspersed Irish districts remained, living the old life-mode, restless and vengeful. The actual labourers remained where they were, and were on the whole no worse off materially, and probably some of them were happier as *villeins* than as serfs.

One can still feel this Norman influence. It hangs almost palpably in the air of some parts of the country, distinctive and unmistakable, chiefly in the east and south-east. In such counties as Kilkenny, where this influence lasted long and was least disturbed, even by the disastrous upheaval of the Reformation,† the very nature of the people is pa-

---

* The Gaelic world had not only 'towns' but 'cities' in the sense of a conglomeration of huts or tents around a monastery. A town in the legal and mercantile sense is a walled-in permanent settlement—without walls it is an open village—with a market and generally a charter and often a trade monopoly. No trade—no town: merely a village or some sort of impermanent kraal, like the mule, 'without pride of ancestry or hope of posterity.'

† Is it necessary to remind ourselves that the Norman invasion, unlike the Tudor invasion, was carried out by Catholics?

tently different to that of the contiguous county of Tipperary. Even the people of south Tipperary, which was more effectively colonised than north Tipperary, appear to me, at any rate, clearly affected by that prolonged foreign reign.

A Norman Centre

Where the invaders established abbeys this influence is most pronounced. I happen to have made a study of one such district, that around the present village of Graiguenamanagh on the River Barrow, in County Kilkenny, the site of a Cistercian Abbey called *De Valle Sancti Salvatoris*, founded by William the Marshal in the twelfth century. Within living memory one could have found almost every necessary craft being still practised in this tiny village— boatbuilding, nailmaking, weaving, bacon-curing, the making of salt, starch and candles, tanning, bootmaking, a small foundry, wheelwrights, carpenters, joiners, tinsmiths, bakers, coopers, quilters, and so on.

In the rich country around the farmhouses have an air rather of Wessex than of Ireland, solid cutstone barns, finely arched, with all the marks of a tradition of good husbandry, such as old trees, straight ditches, orchards and kitchen gardens. And there is all over the land the fragrance of a long memory of stable conditions, so different to the harsh south and west where the generations have lived for centuries from hand to mouth and have only in our time cut free from the gnawing fear of poverty and famine. For the story of many parts of Ireland there are no records: here there are many, rent-rolls and charters that take us back to the middle ages. Nor was this region on the River Barrow fortunate simply because the soil was rich. When the first Cistercians from Wiltshire stood on the hills above the river and saw what they had to cope with they called it 'a place of horror and vast solitude,' for it was dark with wood and scrub and the threat of lawless men.

Or the traveller should visit the modern city of Kilkenny with its beautiful twelfth-thirteenth century cathedral, and its other Norman remains; although its ancient round tower and fragments of a Romanesque church show that it had a pre-Norman life as a religious centre its expansion and civil importance dates from 1192 when the first castle of the Marshals was built. It has flourished ever since and is, so far as I know, the only such town or city that has, like so many English cathedral towns, grown under the wings of abbey and of manor, adapting itself graciously to Time without wholly losing its original quality.

To make another of my forward leaps, the contrast with the ultimate fate of that village and abbey of Graiguena-managh is pointed. This village was far from clustering for shelter under the protecting wings of the old abbey—said by one traveller to have been, even in its ruin, as beautiful as Tintern. It has, in the most amazing, terrifying and thorough fashion, crept over the abbey, stock and stone, built garage and pub and warehouse and shop and stye and police barracks on top of, in and with its fallen stones, so that, to-day, this memorial of Norman civilisation lies like a drowned glory beneath a little Irish village, and no casual traveller would notice anything, until, by halting for a few days, he would gradually become aware of an aura not of our time. Searching, then, he will come upon the poor stones from which it emanates; and, searching deeper, find the Norman spirit still powerful in the na-ture of the people about and in the husbandry of the land.

Norman Exclusivism

The point of the contrast is, ultimately, political. It marks the beginning of the central Irish tragedy. The Normans did not give to the Irish the benefits of their own laws. So little did they realise, as the Danish kings realised when they conquered Britain, that the keystone of a successful colonisation is a blending of races, which is in turn dependent on the rule of equal rights for all before the law, that it was no felony in Norman-Irish law to kill an Irishman. (The fact that it was, in effect, no felony for an Irishman to kill a Norman has nothing to do with the principle of the matter; though Orpen is, no doubt, right in seeing at the root of this fatal error of statesmanship the fact that the Normans, in their ignorance of Ireland, regarded the Irish as uncouth and barbarous, as the Tudors were to do after them.) Since the military conquest was far from complete, for it was firm only in the east, weak in the south, and scarcely touched the north and west, one may imagine the result. Add to this discrimination the greatest weakness of all, that the foreign king lived in another country, was always otherwise engaged—

'and, indeed, in the person of King John, was not morally equipped, either to rule his (Irish) barons with justice or to restrain them from harsh treatment of his Irish subjects.'

By the time of the Reformation a typical village and abbey like this Graiguenamanagh was no longer pure Norman. If Lynch's famous epigram that the Normans became *Hiberniores Hibernicis ipsis* (more Irish than the Irish themselves), is an overstatement, it contains an historical truth—that Ireland, whether Norman or Gaelic, went as much of its own way as 'the alternate neglect and capri-

cious interference' of the *Dominus Hiberniae* would allow
it to go; and, as we know, at the Reformation Ireland
went as it had always gone along the road of the old faith.
Abbeys and cathedral-churches in Britain might then,
with exceptions, continue under the new dispensation. In
Ireland the exception was the other way round. Here an-
archy was always nearer at hand. The abbey was abandoned and neglected and ultimately tumbled in on itself.
As the village throve the abbey vanished. Its influence remains, masked and muffled, a symbol of the incomplete-
ness of the Norman conquest itself. But one need not go
to any such town or village for these symbols. Many a ruined Norman castle, with its sheltering cows, is all that remains of a town whose memory is otherwise only preserved
by local tradition, parchments in a museum, humps of
grass.

Our Norman Blood

The simplest illustration of the masked influence is, of
course, in our surnames. Burkes are Norman De Burgos,
and Fitzgerald, Power, Joyce, Coady, Tracy, Costello, Butler, Barry, and others more Gaelic-seeming, like Mac-
Aveely, are likewise Norman. The late Edmund Curtis,
Professor of History in Dublin University, an authority on
the period, in a cursory study estimated that at least a sev-
enth of the commonest Irish surnames are Norman. Whenever, he said, one meets the round compact head, the pale
complexion, sturdy build, square face, fine nose, falcon
rather than eagle-like, such as we saw in the Irish leader
John Redmond, one meets the true Norman type. The
mental characteristics are emotional control, conservation
of energies, restrained idealism, a certain closeness, frugal
yet open-handed, 'traders rather than industrialists, safe

rather than speculative,' imagination well in hand, a good deal of self-reliance, sometimes vindictive, always stubborn. Curtis thought them *rusé* and full of wile. The strain is now so much mingled and watered that one no more meets a pure Norman than one can find a pure Celt, yet this is not the list of qualities that one would think of when speaking of the more Gaelic parts of Ireland where character is so much more ebullient and unpredictable.

It was the Normans who first introduced the Irish mind to politics. They were our first Home Rulers. They did not think of Ireland as a nation, least of all as their nation, or bother about such symbols as Language, and they had no interest in ancient traditions, but they stood as sturdily for their religion and their land as, in the nineteenth century, an O'Connell for the one and a Davitt for the other; by which time, of course, Norman and Irish were completely commingled. They initiated politics as the word was to be understood in Ireland to the end of the Irish Parliamentary Party in 1922.

The Norman-Irish Merging

The first Irish Parliament met in 1297. In passing acts forbidding Normans to dress or wear their hair long, like the Irish, or to maintain Irish foot-soldiers or *kernes,* and in applying the term 'degenerate English' to such as did, it shows the way the wind was already blowing. They were being merged; it was also felt in London that they were simultaneously too powerful. Both tendencies are illustrated by the two De Burgos of Connacht who frankly rejected feudal law in favour of the old Gaelic law of male succession in order to get possession of their father's lands in Galway and Mayo. They thereby founded the two great lines of the Clanrickard Burkes and the Mayo Burkes who, without any legal title, were lords of the west up to the middle of the sixteenth century—when the Tudor conquerors were to curse and scorn 'the beggarly Burkes' as heartily and bitterly as they ever cursed any Gael. The same thinning of what Curtis aptly calls 'the feudal veneer' might be illustrated by many other examples. It was to check this movement that official after official was sent to Ireland, and in resistance to these the descendants of the first colonists persistently raised the claims of their own native caste to rule Ireland from within. The distance in time is great to Grattan's 'Patriot Parliament,' to the great fight against the legislative Union of Ireland and Great Britain in the eighteenth century, but the sentiment and the technique of those movements have here their common origin.

The native Irish paid no overt attention whatever to these first political *démarches*. But they could not ignore the *fact,* and the fact was to become their deepest inner tension, their abiding obsession—to be summed up as 'the English enemy.' There was not a year, not a month, not a day, in some part or other of the island that this animus was not blown upon and the eyes of the more thoughtful, at least, turned towards the East. For, even if the Irish took no specific interest in Anglo-Irish politics, they were obliged to adapt themselves to its effects. If the Normans tended to become Irishised, the Irish were forced to become more and more feudal. One sees this in the adoption of the feudal right of the son to succeed the father, which virtually changed the Gaelic chiefs, or the 'captains of nations,' or 'lords of countries,' as the English legal phrases called them, into Gaelic barons. One sees the feudalisation of their minds, too, in their introduction of standing armies and mercenaries, chiefly nationalised Norse from the Scottish isles. Apart from the old rule of the chieftain's limited ownership of land their power was thus to become more and more arbitrary. In one way and another the generations (for the process was of the slowest) were obliged, too, to deal with what the eighteenth century called Dublin, the nineteenth called 'Dublin Castle,' and our time calls 'the Government,' and which in all centuries from then to now it is their concern to pacify or to circumvent. In those centuries their technique was one of resistance to the limit, always too local to be effective or lasting, followed by feigned submissions and simulated friendship.

Our Unwise Opportunism

One pauses to consider that one of the fondest Irish delusions is that we are a guileful people. We expect guile from one another as we expect rain from our skies. If, however, we meet guile or rain in other lands we are a little pained. We are especially taken aback if we find that England is either wetter or more wily than Ireland. It is possible that other countries share our delusion and it may be not shock but disappointment which has produced the epithet 'perfidious Albion.' It may seem on the surface that in those frequent submissions exacted by English kings and more or less readily made by the Irish kings, with little intention of implementing them, the English were wasting and the Irish purchasing valuable time. Twice, for example, Richard II came in person to Ireland to receive the homage of the paramount chiefs, in return for which they were in 1395 at last admitted as legal possessors of the land they had inherited—a considerable triumph for them at the period—and against which they, on their side, agreed to surrender lands they had been 'usurping' from the barons. Practically, nothing at all would seem to have happened except that Richard went his way rejoicing. But empires can afford to take their time, and an invaded people cannot. And things did happen beneath the surface. Curtis rightly points out that it is significant that after that imposing and solemn submission of 1395 the greater Irish chiefs dropped the title of 'king,' so that henceforth, for example, MacCarthy is not 'King of Desmond' but 'The MacCarthy More.' The Irish had not surrendered land; but they had surrendered some portion of their minds, their memories, their traditional outlook. As this is a non-political history it is not our business to consider whether it might not have been far better if they had either united and fought, or honestly submitted and settled down with the Norman barons to create a Norman-Irish island to balance against that Anglo-Norman island across the sea: but, since they neither did one thing nor the other, one can only observe that the upshot of it was that they introduced themselves to politics under the worst possible definition and under the worst possible conditions —that is to say, without any intellectual idea or any moral purpose—in a word, opportunistically.

Norman-Gaelic Poetry

The Normans brought other less Grecian gifts to the Irish mind. They brought into the landlocked lagoon of Gaelic literature welcome gushes from the world's seas. From this period come most of the Gaelic translations of European literature that we possess, mainly classical and Arthurian tales and poems—Irish versions of the Romance of the Grail, Marco Polo, Virgil's Æneid, the Trojan Wars, the Odyssey, the mediaeval English romances of Guy of Warwick and Bevis of Hampton, the Travels of Maundeville, the legend of the Minotaur. But the most charming of all their gifts was the elaborate convention of Provençal love-poetry which the Gaelic poets skilfully adapted to their own formal traditions, indeed absorbed into them. Here, as in the early lyrics, is again a perfect synthesis—confined, alas, to this one small field—a synthesis this time between Europe and Ireland, between the graceful formalities of a new society and the wild passions of an old one, greatly exciting in its suggestion of what might have come from a complete wedding of Norman and Gael.

One poem, in fine translation from the Gaelic by Padraic Colum, will give us an example of this new departure:

> O woman, shapely as the swan,
> On your account I shall not die.
> The men you've slain—a trivial clan—
> Were less than I.
>
> I ask me shall I die for these;
> For blossom-teeth and scarlet lips?
> And shall that delicate swan-shape
> Bring me eclipse?
>
> Well shaped the breasts and smooth the skin,
> The cheeks are fair, the tresses free;
> And yet I shall not suffer death,
> God over me.
>
> Those even brows, that hair like gold,
> Those langorous tones, that virgin way;
> The flowing limbs, the rounded heel
> Slight men betray.

Thy spirit keen through radiant mien,
Thy shining throat and smiling eye,
Thy little palm, thy side like foam—
I cannot die.

O woman, shapely as the swan,
In a cunning house hard-reared was I;
O bosom white, O well-shaped palm
I shall not die.

That is but one note or convention out of many. And yet,
perhaps, it may be more than a convention, more than one
move in the game of *amour courtois,* like the movement
of refusal in certain amorous dances that end in fore-
ordained surrender and passion. It may be that there is
something in G. K. Chesterton's comment that this is 'the
hardness of the real Irishman,' for whom love is no game
—as it was not for Dermot MacMurrough who burnt another Ilium for O'Rourke's wife. It may not be just a blind
shot for Chesterton to say that the 'curt, bleak words'
(though bleak is certainly not the right adjective) 'come
out of the ancient Ireland of cairns and fallen kings' and
'a haughty, heathen spirit.' Whether heathen or Christian
there is at any rate a something different about many of
them when set side by side with Provençal verse; as in that
wild poem about the woman torn between two loves, her
poet-lover and her husband, of which Dr. Robin Flower
wrote that

'it is the last in a long series of poems, like the Old Woman
of Beare and Liadain and Cuirithir, in which a figure or a
situation of passion is realised with an absolute and final
intensity. Such poems as these would alone justify the
study of Irish literature, for their like is not to be found

elsewhere, and their disappearance would be a loss not only to Ireland but to the whole world.' *

The Great 'If Only . . .'

It may be said that in recording the effects of the Norman invasion we should also consider what kind of native Irish culture might have developed naturally *if* this brutal interruption had not occurred. I confess that I have felt a strong aversion to these historical hypotheses ever since I came on a book by a philosopher named Renouvier entitled *The Civilisation of Europe as It Might Have Been But Has Not,* based on the theory that were it not for a minor variation introduced at the close of the reign of Marcus Aurelius and affecting the power of Commodus Pertinax and Albinus the victory of Christianity might not have occurred. Nevertheless it is an historical fact, of which note may be taken, that some Irish efforts to reform the church and shape a coherent society were being made just before the Normans came; with some promises of the appurtenances of a coherent society, hitherto lacking or inadequate; such as a proper church-organisation and a fitting church-architecture. In order, however, that these native reformers could have succeeded they would first have required what early Christianity abroad required, to establish a well-knit clerical organisation—that is, a centralised secular arm. Papal Rome could not have controlled Antioch without the Roman legions to enforce its decisions: every church has, at its beginnings, in some degree to be a political church. Before Armagh could control Cork or Limerick the Irish reformers would first have

* The Gaelic anthology of these poems is *Dánta Grádha.* Edited and collected by Tomás O'Rathaile. (Cork, 1926.) Translations in *Love's Bitter Sweet,* by Robin Flower. (Cuala Press. Dublin, 1925.)

needed, likewise, a centralised Irish state, and, in fact, they made some gallant, but quite hopeless efforts in that direction.

Let us take the illustration offered by architecture. The outward mark and measure of the virility of the native spirit are the little Romanesque churches which we find, to-day, hidden here and there among the alders and the nettles; and one or two much later abbeys, like Mellifont, built under foreign supervision, both naturally so and properly so. The proportions of the Romanesque chapels are almost always good; a few are dramatically beautiful; some are barbarous; some are downright crazy. The chancel-arch at Clonmacnoise, for instance, looks as if it had been hacked out with hatchets by masons drunk on poteen and hot with raw flesh. One order of the voussoirs shows a simple chevron and line ornament which, normally, would have appeared as a continuous line or moulding below, and a continuous saw-tooth above; but with a wild wilfulness these builders have rudely turned every second stone upside down! So, we get a jagged bit of moulding, then a jagged bit of chevron, then another jagged bit of moulding, and so on. All I can see, as I look at the extraordinary result, is a bunch of intoxicated masons, rolling on the ground in paroxysms of laughter as they look up at their handiwork; rather like a bunch of drunken undergraduates who, with infinite pains and misplaced ingenuity, have succeeded in making a statue of the founder of their college stand on its head. At the other end of the scale the arch and gable at Clonfert is the work of genius.

As for the abbeys they are now in such a ruinous and despoiled state that it is not easy to measure their value or even date what is left. The chancel-window at Jerpoint is suggestively delicate. The groined roof at Mellifont seems

to be late. There is exceedingly little sculpture or carving
or tile-work by comparison with the continent. One goes
about among the wet grass and the thistles pointing to
fragments. Even so there is enough to make one say that
these reformers and these artists, imported or native—it
makes no matter; all ideas get imported from somewhere
—given more time, and left undisturbed, *might* have
dragged Ireland into the main stream of European civilisation. One may not say that they would certainly have
done so. One may not even say that it is likely. History
records the facts of a matter. The fact is that they did not.

A Racial Weakness?

Is this a condemnation of the Irish as a race? Does it
point to a racial weakness? Indubitably. In saying so I
shall be charged by some with lack of patriotism, and by
others with too much of it—i.e. with 'racialism': That is to
say, with explaining historical events in terms of racial
characteristics instead of in terms of the material circumstances that condition these events. I shall be told that the
Irish could not be blamed for not being in the European
swim at the date of the Norman invasion; that it does not
in the least matter if one country makes its achievements
five hundred years later than another; that history is not
an obstacle race; that the simple fact is that all civilisation
in Europe came up from the south and east and that Ireland was at the end of the queue; that racialism inevitably
leads us to pass silly moral judgements on countries for
not doing things which it was physically impossible for
them to have done; like despising the East for not having
Gothic churches or bacon-and-eggs; that the Irish could not

have been blamed for not doing for themselves what the Normans had to do for them.

The anti-racialist will say that the actual picture was something like this:—Somewhere on the eastern Mediterranean a divine Quartermaster had, for centuries, been handing out the seeds of life to Europe. He had said, 'Greece forward!', and Greece replied, 'Present, sir,' and filled her basket, and planted and grew. He and Greece then said, in unison, 'Rome!', and Rome said, 'Coming up,' and they passed on the old seed, and some new seed, and Rome planted and grew. He and Greece and Rome then said in unison, 'Byzantium!', and Constantinople and Dalmatia and the Balkans and, in due course, the Venetians, had come forward with their baskets to receive the seed. And, say these critics, all the time little Ireland was away off down the line, peeping out hungrily, with eager eyes and trembling hands. By the time the Quartermaster got to Ireland it was a case of too little and too late. 'Too late' because of the Norman invasion. But she *would* have got it had the Normans never come.*

* A small but significant illustration of this 'too little and too late' cropped up recently in an interesting Irish law-case about the public ownership of fisheries. The greatest living authority on ancient Irish law, Professor Daniel Binchy, in giving evidence to show that there was no public ownership of fisheries in pre-Norman times in Ireland quoted, among other examples, a royal (i.e. Irish royal) charter bestowing fishing-rights on a medieval Irish monastery. Counsel for the State, who was attempting to maintain that there *was* public ownership in pre-Norman times—the Irish Government has, for some years, been attempting to expropriate some of these privately owned fisheries—pointed out that the monks appeared to be given, under this charter, ownership according to the Norman right called 'free alms': in other words he wished to make the point that the charter could *not* be pre-Norman, and so not relevant. (Professor Binchy's reply to this was that the monks probably wrote the charter themselves—the local king not particularly caring what formulas were employed.) What this little straw shows is that the wind had begun to blow some feudal ideas into Ireland even before the Normans came. There, in Ireland, in other words, were already a few monks from Britain or Normandy, the first ripples of the flood that was to come, some thirty years later, but not in peace but bloodshed with the full Norman invasion.

The image of the races queuing up is suggestive and I should not hesitate to give it to a child at school as a picture of how Europe grew; but it is far from being a complete or accurate picture, and I should fill it out in many ways, for in several essentials it is false.

Thus, the main implication of the picture is that there are no such things as racial characteristics. There is nothing but geography (with climate and all the rest of it) and the effects of time, and time-lags. If there are no such things as racial characteristics then all I can say is that Bernard Shaw writes exactly like a Pole, and there is no such thing as a Jew, and anybody could have seen that Mussolini was an Englishman. The anti-'racialist'—which is merely a tag-word anyway—counters by admitting what he calls 'local variation,' or 'local colouring,' or 'local accent'; which is to admit the fact of racial characteristics once for all. The truth is that races do not start equal and identical any more than men. A cat and tiger may have stemmed from the one origin in pre-history. By the time we know them in history the cat is a cat; the tiger is a tiger; the Teuton is a Teuton; and the Celt is a Celt.

Racial Genius

Races, furthermore, are not passive recipients. They are a collective will. They have urges and instincts and desires of their own. They are not going to take that seed, each one, and do the same identical thing with it. Let me give an example. The Romans took over Greek architecture and for hundreds of years—so obsessed were they by its dominant trabeation—they kept the entablature distinct from the arch. (See all the Roman amphitheatres, in which the several and separate arches do the work but the emphasis is on the decorative column and the entablature.) *That they could combine the arch with the column never occurred to them.* In their great engineering works, such as aqueducts, they did spring the arches from piers; but in domestic architecture, with the exception of one insignificant example, at Pompeii, they never sprang the arches from the columns. They were so devoted to the idea that the entablature must be above the column that when, as sometimes happened, the arch had perforce to rise above the level of the column, they stuck, with fantastic logic, on top of the column, and the capital, another bit of pier, and ran an entablature all around the four sides of it, and *then* permitted the arches to occur! But it was the triumph of the Byzantine architects, first seen at work at Diocletian's palace at Spalato, in Dalmatia, to spring the arches directly from the column. Why? We do not know. From this simple action, which seems as obvious to us now as that Columbus should naturally arrive in America if he sailed westwards, the whole of modern architecture stemmed. Even after Italy discovered this trick why is it that, in Rome, from the 4th century to the 11th, the builders clung to the simple form of the basilica? To the flat roof, the simple apse, the simple stresses, when, away down in the Harouan desert of Syria men had, for hundreds of years, been constructing domes? Local colouring? No! Local genius, rather.

In short, then, we have to have a name for such groups of men with their own distinctive gifts and desires and lacks. We call them what they became—races of men. 'By their fruits we shall know them.'

The Racial Struggle

Nor did the races of the world stand in a queue, like well-drilled soldiers. It was all rather more like a scramble, where first come was first served, and where one of the first things each did with the gifts given to him was not to take the spade and plar t but to take the spade and hit the other fellow with it. And each race had to expect this as part of the hazards of existence, and fight off its enemies while it built and worked. It had to organise. It had to cope with earthquakes, internecine war, internal dissensions, new and sometimes dangerous ideas or 'heresies,' rebuild and rebuild after each disaster. History *is* the record of an obstacle race. To know that this is how races achiéve all one has to do is to stand on the Janiculum Hill in Rome, and look over its vast perspective of history, of ruin, of decay from war and pestilence, with buildings built time and again on and with the ruins of former buildings. To go into some of its famous monuments is to see layer upon layer of death and resurrection.

Invasion Inevitable

Now, who were the Irish that they should ask longer time and more undisturbed conditions than they got? They had got the seeds; as we have seen they made them flower, splendidly, when Europe was in the Dark Ages; and then they stopped watering and pruning and manuring and transplanting; and the harvest withered and the heath crept back foot by foot over the cultivated land. It is quite true that this island was placed by God and Nature at the tip of the continental archipelago, far from all that had emerged, and had been for centuries travelling westward, from Mycenae and Thebes, from Athens and Byzantium, from Rome and Venice and Lombardy, across the Gulf of Lyons, through Angoulême and Perigueux and Limoges to the rim of Europe. But is it really true that its people were awaiting all that 'with eager eyes and trem-

bling hands'? It seems, rather, that somebody had to per-
form some forcible-feeding, or blood-transfusion; that the
Norman invasion, or some invasion, had to be. That it
occurred is an historical fact which nobody doubts. That
it, or some such transfusion, had to occur is as undeniable.
No major historical event is an accident. That it brought
great gifts to Ireland is patent. To suggest that it was
a pity it happened and that something more interesting
might have happened if it had not happened is to raise
an utterly futile hypothesis which leaves one beating the
air, and groping with might-have-beens, and propounding
all sorts of unanswerable questions, such as 'Why did they
not beat back the Normans?', or 'Why did they not cope
with them?' And to end up, if one is persistent enough,
with a history of 'The Civilisation of Ireland as It Has
Not Been but Might Have,' had Dervorgilla's nose been
an inch longer so that MacMurrough (who quarrelled
with his neighbours over her) would not have invited
the Normans at all. Hard cases make bad law and excul-
pations make poor history. The Irish had had room and
room enough, time and time enough. They made a marvellous start with their romantic literature, and in and
after the fifth century they laid their hands greedily on
the heritage of Rome and Greece. By the tenth century
they had allowed themselves to fossilise, and after it lived
like the grasshopper, unready for the storm. They had
seven hundred years, from the coming of Christianity to
the coming of the Normans, during which they might have
organised church and state. They failed to do it. One may
imagine the God of History waiting and waiting and waiting, generation after generation, century after century,
and finally taking up his pen, writing them off and closing
his book with a disgusted snap.

Neither can we seriously indulge the wish that, since the Norman invasion had to occur, it would have better occurred more thoroughly, and that it would have been no more a shame or loss but a great gain for this island to have been properly conquered than it was for the island next door. That 'if only' is another hypothesis. The comparative failure of the Normans was also an inevitable result of the Irish character and of the Irish geographical disadvantage of being at the end of the queue. One of Arnold Toynbee's themes is the effect of what he calls Challenge and Response. The Challenge (before the Normans) was not great enough. The Response was proportionate. The Happy Isle was too happy. The Challenge of the Normans was not great enough. The Response was proportionate. If the Happy Isle was not as happy as it had been it was still too happy to stir itself sufficiently either to throw the Normans out or to blend with them for the creation of a fine hybrid society. Conversely the Normans in Britain did not feel an acute Challenge from Ireland. So they all jogged along like a not particularly well-matched man and wife who are neither uncomfortable enough to break the home nor comfortable enough to feel the urge to make a complete success of it.

There is a great deal about Ireland, then and now, that stems from this. It is a very pleasant feather-bed. It is one of the most pleasant beds in the world to lie on, and the challenge of the world is dulled by the falling rain, and by distance, and by the thought which atrophies all old nations, unless they strive deliberately against it, that the ambition of the younger ones is always getting people into a lot of unnecessary trouble. And anyway, they think, turning over for another snooze, 'We have heard it all before.' It is simply next-door to impossible to stir modern Irishmen by quoting to them the examples of other countries. Whether from inertia, or from arrogance, or from a too-great sense of security they refuse to bother their heads about the example of other lands. So it has always been, away back and back through the centuries.

The result is one of the greatest puzzles in the history of mankind: that which Toynbee has called the 'abortive western Celtic civilisation.' Why did the Irish bud never flower to fullness? Why did Irish art, architecture, writing, philosophy, and all the rest run down like a clock that stops? Why, after the great efflorescence of the 6th and later centuries did the tree go barren? There is no other answer than the racial character, with all its virtues and all its weaknesses, that had developed down the centuries. As to what had formed that character nobody will ever know now. Naturally geography and so on helped to form it. Nature and nurture combined in that formation. The Celt had some original genetic distinctiveness of his own and the surrounding circumstances affected that distinctiveness. All a historian can do is to take the 'specimen' as and when he finds it, in historical times, and describe it; and since he must have a name for it, he must call it a strain or breed or race, and he must call that strain whatever it is commonly called in history: in our case, the Celtic strain or race.

He has one final answer to those who still insist that, in giving praise or blame to the Celts for doing or not doing something, we must never say that they did or did not do this something because they were Celts; but merely say they did or did not do it because of material environment. This is his final answer:—'Why then did not the Celts surmount environment? True, they were at the end of the queue. But why did they not turn the queue around?

China was as far from Greece and the Mediterranean, yet she formed a continuous culture of her own.' To this there can be no reply.

It is, therefore, proper and historical, to accept the existence of a well-developed Celtic character, autonomous, subject only to itself, fully responsible for its own behaviour, and fit to plead at the bar of history to the charge of having lost a great chance.

The Religious Strain

THE potentially most fruitful bond between Norman and Irish was religion. Unfortunately it had no direct political carry-over. The Normans had Norman priests, the Irish had Irish priests. The famous Statutes of Kilkenny, 1366, the most outstanding Norman effort to keep 'the two nations' apart, had, among other things, excluded Irish clerics from English houses and benefices. But religion alone could never have united the people, never have over-ridden their other, deeper loyalties: the Catholics of the Pale, that secure English land in the East radiating out from Dublin, would, for example, never have joined the rest of the island in a Catholic enterprise against England. Religion alone would not have been enough to bind even the Irish. When, in the sixteenth century, the Desmonds of the south rose in a war of revolt which took on the nature of a Holy War, the O'Neills of the north rode on the English side against them. It is futile to consider whether what we nowadays call 'nationality' would, without religion, have united the Irish since the term meant as yet nothing to them. They still had only the old sentimental feeling of otherness but no political concept of nationalism.

What religion did effect, however, was of paramount importance in modern Irish orientations. It turned the Irish mind away from England to Rome and Spain. That movement outward was to do much to enlarge the Irish mind, to give it something of a world-outlook, although, ultimately, the association of religion and political resistance to Britain was to merge both in a manner not very satisfactory to either.

The Church Splits

But this is merely to read one of our forward-pointing signposts at a cross-roads in history. Having read the warning inscription (and glanced at the rough country ahead) let us lower our eyes to the fourteenth century and look around the terrain. We have come far from the first stages of the invasion under Henry II and see ahead the bulky shadow of Henry VIII. The Irish Church has formally accepted the Irish monarch as *Dominus Hiberniae* (from the time of Henry II: Synod of Cashel, 1171). 'This synod put the coping-stone on the long work of reform but accompanied it with submission to the English king.' It regulated marriages, baptisms, tithes; established finally that long-needed episcopal and parochial organisation; ended native liturgies—'The divine offices shall be celebrated according to the use of the Church of England'; it submitted to Henry. Within one hundred and fifty years, however, in 1317, at the time of the invasion of Ireland by Edward Bruce of Scotland, a combination of Irish chiefs has to send a Grand Remonstrance to the Pope at Avignon, charging the English kings with (among secular cruelties and injustices) the wrongs done to the Irish Church. That date may mark the clear beginning of the split. It develops when the Papacy intervened to prevent the operation of that Statute of Kilkenny which differentiated between Irish priest and Norman priest, an intervention which had the natural effect of attracting the sympathies of the greatest number towards Rome.

The situation could not develop clearly for over two hundred years after that because the Church in Ireland, taken as a whole, became more and more disunited and disorganised. On the eve of the Reformation it had fallen back into a state of 'spiritual and intellectual stagnation.' 'Abuses of every description prevailed.' '. . . Some of (the clergy) were openly immoral and many of them had not sufficient learning to preach or instruct their flocks.'*

Faith and Fatherland

It was not until the sixteenth century, when partly under the pressure of the Reformation and partly under the effective evangelising work of the mendicant orders who, when scattered by the suppression of their houses, went far and wide preaching at once loyalty to Rome and revolt against the English, that religion began to be identified, however ambiguously, with patriotic resistance.

Nothing, to risk an Irish bull, could be more illuminating than this ambiguity. For the first real Catholic uprising was led, not by the Irish, but by one of the most pow-

---

* The first two of these quotations are from *Church and State in Tudor Ireland*, R. Dudley Edwards. (London, 1935.) The third is from MacCaffrey: *History of the Catholic Church from the Renaissance to the Revolution*, as quoted by Edwards. The whole of Edwards' Introduction should be read, but I think he is unfair to blame the Normans for so many purely Irish evils. Thus, Edwards: 'It was the Normans who introduced armour and stone fortresses. It was through the Normans that they (the Irish) began to burn churches and despoil their enemies.' Alas, they despoiled themselves let alone their (foreign) enemies hundreds of years before the Normans came; and was it not rather weak of them if they did see a Norman burn a church and said, 'What a good idea!' Doubtless the Normans and the Irish learned both good and bad from each other. It is tiresome when nations blame one another for their own faults.

erful of the old Norman families—the southern Desmonds
—and it arose, in the first place, out of economic pressure.
Necessity had locked them into the Irish system: they had
come to depend for their great power and revenue on
their Gaelic tenants who, in the characteristic fashion of
the period, lived outwardly by feudal and inwardly by
Gaelic loyalties and customs. When Gerald, the fourteenth
earl of Desmond, was held prisoner in London for his failure to suppress this Gaelic life-mode and pay the Queen
her full feudal dues, his cousin Sir James Fitzmaurice got
himself elected captain of his people and went to the continent to raise a great Catholic confederacy, backed by
Philip II and the Pope, against the oppressions of the English. He returned to Ireland in 1579 with some small aid
from Spain and a Bull from the Pope which declared Elizabeth deprived of both her kingdoms. That date, 1579, is
the operative date for the effective beginning of a new,
and thenceforward indissoluble merger of two ideas whose
slogan has ever since powerfully dominated the Irish mind
—Faith and Fatherland.*

The Desmond revolt was crushed bloodily. It was followed by one of the first of several big Plantations. These
have to be mentioned because they meant a further cross-
breeding, a further dilution of Celtic blood. What other
reasons, hidden in the mists of time, there may be for the
many differences in character between the peoples of various parts of Ireland one cannot tell. The Norman strain in
and about Kilkenny and Carlow may not alone account
for the individual quality of those counties; the Danish
background may not alone explain Wexford; the Scottish
infusion Antrim; nor may it wholly explain the qualities

* For a brilliant and moving account of Fitzmaurice's war the reader
should not fail to read *The Celtic Peoples and Renaissance Europe*, by
David Mathew.

of the Cork people that settlers such as Sir Walter Raleigh brought in a transfusion of Devon and Somerset blood. These mixtures did occur and would have had their effects. And as time goes on and cross-breeding flourishes, we will have to agree that too many strains and influences have been woven into the tapestry of the Irish mind for anybody to disentangle them all.

Religion has thus, at the end of a long and tangled period, made Norman and Irish comrades in distress if in nothing else. But there was, as we must have seen, much else. Religion did not and could not do this unaided. It was welded with politics and not unaffected by economic stress. It became, in Fitzmaurice's hands, a standard for a common dissatisfaction with English rule, the first metaphor, the first symbol, of an emergent bud of nationalism.

III · THE BRANCHES

Political History

1556   *First Plantations or Colonisations.*

1586   *Collapse of Desmond Insurrection. Plantation of Munster. A peasant tenantry begins to emerge.*

1592   *First Irish University founded.*

1603   *Collapse of Tyrone (O'Neill) Insurrection. Plantation of Ulster. End of the old Gaelic 'State.'*

1652   *Cromwellian Plantations.*

1691   *End of Williamite wars. More confiscations.*

1700   *The 'Bad Century' begins. Death of Gaelic literature. The Penal Laws. Rise of Anglo-Irish culture.*

1791   *The United Irishmen. Wolfe Tone. The Rebel emerges as a type.*

1801   *Legislative Union of Great Britain and Ireland.*

1829   *Daniel O'Connell wins Emancipation for the Catholics. Rise of modern Irish Democracy. Political power of the Priest begins.*

1841   *The Young Irelanders. Modern Irish writing begins.*

1875   *Rise of Charles Stewart Parnell. The peasant tenantry strengthen their position.*

1916   *The last insurrection.*

1922   *Founding of the Irish Free State.*

1949   *Independence achieved.*

The New Peasantry

A MODERN Irish critic once suggested that the three dominant notes of the Irish consciousness are Land, Religion
and Nationality. (As will be seen I count five such notes,
or branches.) So far, in this history of the Irish consciousness we have seen only the faint outlines of Religion and
Nationalism coming to the surface of the pool, though
mere gleams, indeed, that, at the time, nobody could have
christened. Land, land-hunger, land-passion, land-love and
the author and creature of that love, the peasant, have
as yet made no appearance. As I have said, the literature
of the old Gaelic world did not—to use a modern word—
feature the simple folk. It had no Langland. It shows no
interest in common folk.

A Rent-System

The first people to proclaim even an interest in them
were not native Irish but invading English who were
shocked at their condition—though, to be sure, a political
interest urged this human interest, and what mainly dis-
pleased these colonists no doubt was that these poor flies,
as they called them, were so caught in the web of oppres-
sion of the native chiefs (as indeed they, by now, were) as
to be undetachable from their schemes. It was still true
that the small 'tenants' were much put upon by their lords.

87

Under the old Gaelic system they had been at least to some degree independent; under this latter-day half-Gaelic half-feudal system they had hardly any moral (or immoral) compensations—such as a share in the spoils—for the increasing exactions of their chieftains. The 'tenant' had once been content to entertain fighting-men quartered on him, or give military service himself: when it happened too often, when it seemed to him part and parcel of his general struggling insecurity, he would have welcomed a fixed rent, as in the nineteenth century his descendants certainly did. He was offered exactly this by the Queen's deputy, Bingham, in 1585, under a scheme known as the Composition of Connaught. Thereby every man was to agree to pay 10s. per quarter of arable land per annum to his lord in lieu of the old erratic payments in service. The lord, in his turn, Norman and Irish alike, was to pay a fixed rent to the Government in Dublin. If one refuses to regard Irish history from any other standpoint than that of 'seven-hundred-years-of-slavery,' if nothing is ever to be accepted as a *fait accompli* however unjust in its origins, whether the Danish, Norman, Tudor or Cromwellian colonisations, then it is, of course, another foul injustice to have thus exacted rent from Irishmen for their own native soil. The small farmers of Connaught seem to have been eager for the scheme and all historians are agreed that it was equitable.

One would, in any case, naturally expect that the common people would be the first to weary of the long and, to them, pointless struggle. They would have appreciated what the great Dan O'Connell, the emancipator of his people, said to an old man breaking stones by the road: 'Whatever happens, you will still be breaking stones.' The sixteenth-century English observers, at least, were quite satisfied, again not unnaturally, that 'the common Irish people have desired to leave their own lords and live under the English if they might'; and even claimed that these drudges were in favour of the Plantations that drove their chiefs to the bush:

'they who live by their labours, and are yet hardly suffered by their unruly idle swordsmen to live in safety, or to enjoy of that which they get by their own labours, so much as to sustain their lives, expect to be relieved by the due execution of the laws. . . .'

Not that one accepts such claims as facts, and the contemporary drudge the world over was probably no better off in his day.

Old Princes and New Peasants

There exists from the century following a most interesting document, a prose and verse satire in Gaelic called *The Parliament of Clan Thomas,* which throws a sharp light on what the upper classes of Gaelic society must have felt about the common folk from time immemorial, and were now to feel with an increasing bitterness as their own fortunes dwindled. The author or authors of this satire, evidently products of the old aristocratic bardic schools, adopt a form of heavy irony to flail the rising upstart 'boors.' For within the sixty odd years between the Composition of Connaught (1585) and 1650 when this satire was probably written, the old aristocratic world finally collapsed and the common people set themselves to make the best of the new world. The rise of all common folk is likely to be none too pleasant to watch. To leap forward yet once again we have seen the common folk of Ireland in our own day rise like the beanstalk out of the Revolution of 1922 and their behaviour is often very unpleasant to watch. In the seventeenth century, to use a vulgarism, the old aristocratic Gaelic order 'could not take it,' and one finds it easy enough to sympathise with them.

In this satire they have invented a hateful ancestor for the rising 'boors,' one Thomas, son of Putridpelt, son of Dragonmaggot, son of Beelzebub. With ponderous sarcasm they put into his mouth, and into the mouths of his bestial followers, every sort of revolutionary idea that the authors hate: such as that every member of Clan Thomas must set himself to plough—thus wiping out the old pastoral life on which Gaelic society had always been based; or, again—

'Cleave close together; populate farmsteads and townlands for yourselves; have neither lord nor master but your own selves; make the land dear for the nobility; put brown and red and blue on your clothes, wear collars and ruffs and gloves, and always use half-spurs, half-pillions and pommels.'

The author's hate is evident in many passages.

'Upstart Boors!'

'They (the boors) spent their lives during the reign of every king, waiting on the nobles, in which manner they existed till the time of Elizabeth, daughter of Henry, the eighth king of that name, and during her reign they were in truth full of spunk and swelled head, pride and impudence, because of their abundant prosperity and plenty'—

which takes us back directly to the date of the Composition of Connaught and indicates how much the Gaelic chiefs loathed its ordinances. Or there is this interesting passage, with its important four final words, summarising the history of all the common folk from antiquity to those topsy-turvy days of the sixteenth and seventeenth century:

'Clan Thomas spent their time merrily, well-fed and with light minds, as Saint Patrick had ordained for them. They did not (the author admits with satisfaction) use savoury succulent foods nor sweet intoxicating drinks, nor clean well-fitting clothes, but crude canvas shirts, slimy coarse swallow-tail coats woven of the foul hair of puck goats and other animals, stinking boots of untanned leather, crooked long-lappeted caps without make or shape, bedunged bare, rusty, slippery clogs; while, as Patrick had bade them, they watched and waited, served and ploughed and slaved for the nobles and gentry of Christian kind during the reign of every king (he means every Gaelic king) from time immemorial, and they were craven before the kingly decrees, *as was their duty.*'

(This is the poor old Church being dragged, as usual, into the 'class-war.')

That satire marks a most important date in Irish social history—the breach between the ordinary peasant folk and the old native aristocracy, whom, one can only presume, they now thought of as failures. There are other documents which indicate that the recriminations were mutual and savage.*

The occasion of this section, the fixed rent practice introduced by the Composition of Connaught, has at all times since been in the foreground of the peasant's mind. Over and over again from the seventeenth century on ob-

* The passages from *Clan Thomas* are quoted from translations in *The Bell* (Dublin; monthly), by Francis MacManus, beginning September 1943. A complete edition awaits publication by the Irish Texts Society; Editor, the Rev. H. McAdoo.

servers remark that if the tenant could pay his rent and
live he counted himself a happy man. The thirst for security is, above all things, the great obsession of the peasant
mind. And, in a long view, a deceptive obsession. The Irish
tenants who compounded for a fixed rent in the sixteenth
century won security and, in a sense, they won a degree
of independence; but it was independence only of their
chiefs' exactions, not a general independence as freemen.
In the old system they were, as we have seen from our
brief consideration of the Old Irish system, effectual freeholders: that is, they held their land, incontestably, for
three generations at the least. In the new system they were
leaseholders; that is, they held their land from year to
year.

Tenant Not Yeoman

Now, if there is anything in English life to correspond
with the old Gaelic system it would be that which created
the yeoman class, those who from 1430 onward were considered entitled to vote, i.e. farmers who worked their own
freehold when it was worth forty shillings a year in the
values of the time—anything around £100 to-day—and who
were known thereafter as the forty-shilling freeholders.
(In the nineteenth century when at long last the vote was
given to Irish Catholics only the forty-shilling freeholders
were emancipated.) That old Gaelic 'farmer' had a vote,
knew what it was and exercised it in elections. This new
Irish farmer had no vote. He was a mere tenant, politically
unfree, not a yeoman or freeman. And tenants—which, in
Ireland, effectually speaking means 'peasants'—may have
many wonderful and attractive qualities, and preserve valuable things in life, such as kindness, humour, charity,

oral traditions, fellowship, a sense of wonder, even a sense
of the magic of the world: but his virtues are always
passive virtues, not the active virtues of initiative, direction, or invention. He will never, for example, contribute
generative or revolutionary ideas. These come from elsewhere. Thus, as Mr. Christopher Dawson has pointed out
to us, it was not the 'peasant' or 'tenant' spirit but the yeoman spirit which established English democracy, that tradition which kept alive there the sturdy English spirit of
popular independence by never allowing the classes to get
water-tight. The yeoman and the burgesses have always
been the stiffening in that prolonged fight for popular lib-
erties, never the tenantry.

So it was with this first flicker of the rise of a tenant class
in Ireland, which the old bardic aristocratic mind sati-
rised so furiously and understandably. Since we now know
that they were, in time, to develop, under the leadership
of the great Dan O'Connell, into the raw material of modern Irish democracy we can afford to welcome their arrival
—we have no option, like the lady who said to Carlyle, 'I
have decided to accept the universe.' But let us not be
sentimental or romantic about them, and certainly not
joyously enthusiastic in any kind of modern socialistic way,
for their's must have been for centuries a rather hopeless
kind of mind, and they would never have arrived anywhere without the leadership of the townsmen. Even when
O'Connell was leading them two hundred and fifty years
later he cried that nobody would ever 'believe the species
of *animals* with whom he had to carry on his warfare
against the common enemy.' This tenant mind is fast dis-
appearing in Ireland, mainly because almost all farmers
are now freeholders. Having won not a short-term security
but a long-term security, they now have every opportunity

to become as independent-minded as any yeoman, and as politically creative.

Loss and Gain

But this is not, perhaps I should stress, a wholly political comment. It involves culture too. I have mentioned, and should again stress that the folk-mind is the repository of its own riches. It was not to the rich big farmers but to the poor little men that Yeats went for the ancient memory which would seem to be their compensation on earth for their earthly misery. It is the poor and simple of heart who come closest to the gods, cherish them long after they have been cast out elsewhere. The tenant, or Irish peasant, is the child of time. He is its guardian and its slave. He will preserve for centuries dull and foolish habits that those who neither love nor fear time or change will quickly cast aside; but he will also preserve dear, ancient habits that like wine and ivory grow more beautiful and precious with age, all jumbled with the useless lumber in that dusty cockloft which is his ancestral mind.

The reformer, and the peasant is most often in the end his own reformer, foolishly takes a broom and sweeps it all out together in one heap like a ship discarding its ballast; and this seems to be inevitable, for he has no personal knowledge as to what is good or what is useless in his own ways, and knows only his ways, and if you change his ways you have taken the bottom out of his bag. When the poor, rent-paying peasant begins to live like a yeoman farmer his memory foreshortens: it is no longer an ancestral memory, it is merely a personal memory, which dies with him. In one generation folk can change into farmer —or into shopkeeper or civil servant for that matter. You then talk to him about 'the good people' and he will say, 'Ah, yes, I often remember when I was a young lad,' or, 'I often remember my mother to do so and so,' and it all means nothing to him because his life is no longer part of that ancient pattern. It is therefore futile to talk of reviving or of preserving rural ways, in the sense in which people like Mr. Massingham use the word, unless one is also prepared to revive or retain the worst rural ways. And nobody on earth wants that, certainly nobody in Ireland, least of all our landed folk whose whole ambition is to alter that rural way, to make it more and more modern, scientific, profitable and comfortable . . . and to Jericho with 'the good old days' and ways that were so often the bad old days and ways for those who endured them.

The Tenants' Fate

I had better clarify all this by recording the miserable fate of these 16th century commoners of the land in the 17th and 18th century. They did not prosper. But they held on with a tenacity that is the most moving and astonishing spectacle in the whole Irish story. For these centuries, through generation after generation, starving not by thousands but by millions, falling into the earth like the dung of cattle, weeping and cursing as they slaved, patient alike under the indifference of God and of their masters, they clung to their wretched bits of land with a savage fierceness, clung as it were by their bleeding finger-nails. (Nor is the image of finger-nails wholly a metaphor: I have seen, even so late in the day as my own boyhood, an old man in West Cork bringing earth in a bucket and spreading it with his bare hands in the clevvy of a rock.) We can only presume that this tenacity is a common phenomenon among peasants the world over, and that Chinese peasants, say, have likewise clung to their flooded fields, through famines and wars. I cannot believe that any race has held on more bitterly than the Irish. To-day their children's children reap the reward. The rent-rolls of the 17th century record, for many a townland, the names of Papishes—that is wretched, dispossessed creatures, living on a quarter-acre of rotten sod—who, to-day, own snug farms in that same place whence the lords who were their masters and, in all justice, often were their patrons and pitying friends, have died away, been burned out, or willingly emigrated, scornfully leaving them to 'their fate.' That epic of a peasant Israel is in the blood and bones of every Irishman; as inflammable as petrol; so that even when we are most bored, or utterly sick of the extravagances and crudities of Irish nationalism, we have to sympathise, and we try again to understand. I suppose that even the most urbane and civil Irishman could, and will if he is wise, acknowledge that there is in him a vestigial angel or devil that, in propitious circumstances, is capable of turning him into a hero or a savage at the memory of what his fathers endured.

The Tenants' Triumph

Let us carry the story on still farther. It was quite late in the 19th century before these peasant-farmers first began to jack the load, slowly and creakingly, off their backs. That was the period of the Land Struggle under Davitt and Parnell. The Land Act of 1881 fixed their rents, hitherto variable at the landlord's will. An Act of 1885 began their emancipation; it lent them five million pounds to purchase their farms over a period of forty-nine years.

Later Land Acts increased the sum by thirty millions, and then by a hundred millions, and so speeded up the process that in our time the Irish peasant has at last become an independent yeoman farmer owning the ground he tills.

But our business in this book is to consider not what the Irish peasantry endured, now an old and rather exhausted story, but to consider what they produced. Well, these common folk of the land reproduced themselves: they produced a breed of men, a stock as we call it, and many wild aberrants, or 'sports' as gardeners say, scattered now over the face of the earth in that widespread Irish *diaspora* which the world knows. The 'Land' is there to see at the end of it all, farms and homes, their own at last, yeoman's land, in good heart, though the homes are still shockingly far from the comfort that so much endurance deserved and the fields far from being as productive as they could be. They produced other kinds of stock, well-bred over the centuries, such as horses among the best in the world. They preserved up to our own and our children's day, a folk-lore of imaginative power, some humour, a vivid colour, and much variety. They maintained, up to the middle of the 19th century, a popular song-literature which I think it safest to leave to a French scholar to assess, for in Ireland the subject is controversial and some over-rate and some under-rate these verses and songs that are sung or read now only by a very few, or with a self-conscious patriotism.

'The *chant populaire* of Ireland' says Vendryes, 'is of a special importance, due, first to its natural beauty which makes the songs well worth the attention of any music-lover. They have a freshness and spontaneity of feeling, and a delicacy and exactness of expression which ranks them beside the most touching creations of this art . . .

Voltaire has observed that the *chant populaire* is generally rather melancholy. In these Irish songs there is little
of the gaiety, joy or sprightliness that we find in the
French popular airs of the 18th century. Though that
pretty air called *An Maidrín Rua* (The Little Red Fox),
as sung in Munster, is as merry as, for instance our *Com-
père Guilleri*. The music of these songs is of value solely
for its melody. It is not choral music. Musically gifted as
the Irish people are they must give the palm to such foreign peoples as the Germans, the Czechs and the Russians
who have a natural sense of harmony.'

Otherwise, largely because of repression, it has to be
admitted that rural ways and the rural way persisted in
Ireland at a very much lower level than in Britain. It
would be hard, for example, to imagine a book like
George Sturt's *The Wheelwright's Shop* coming out of
Ireland. Because of colonisations and wars and persecu-
tions there is no *physical* continuity in Ireland like to the
physical continuity in Britain, i.e. no ancient villages,
with 'mossed cottage-trees,' old inns, timbered houses,
cropped greens. Handcrafts survive only in the simplest
needs—turf-baskets, churns, farming implements, a few
kitchen utensils.* We have, that is, a sturdy peasantry in
an unfurnished countryside. Britain has a well-furnished
countryside but no peasantry. Our racial memory is,
then, very, very old; but in the foreground of it there is
infinitely more of 'the ancient blinded vengeance and the
wrong that amendeth wrong' than there is of the happy
life. Most of our physical embodiments of the past are
ruins, as most of our songs are songs of lament and defiance. There is therefore far less reason here for the peas-

---

* See Estyn Evans, *The Irish Heritage*. As far as I know the only comprehensive book on this subject.

ant to hang on to the rural way, or for the townsman to idealise it; when he does so it is always for what is called 'spiritual reasons.' The simplest illustration of all this is the fact that there is no Country Cult in Ireland —magazines appealing to the townsman's nostalgic dreams of life in the country—no *Countryside, Countryman, Countrygoer, Country Life.* There is, simply, nowhere for people of civilised tastes to live in the country except in 'The Big House,' and the latest census returns show that even the country people themselves have long been drifting towards the towns.

The Drift from the Land

That drift has never been properly understood. It has been explained in social terms—the young people getting dissatisfied, the country too dull. The true explanation is political; though, nowadays, everything 'political' is called 'social.' It is true that no Irish farm can support more than the eldest son and his family: the rest *must* emigrate to the towns. Undoubtedly, also, country-life is unattractive. But behind these things lies the larger fact that in the towns there has been going on, for generations, a political fight identical to the fight the peasant has waged for centuries on the land.

The peasants' sons and grandsons and great-grandsons in the towns and cities were in a worse position than their fathers in the fields. They had nothing to hang-on to. The rotten sod, bad as it is, is more solid than the rotten slum. The farm landlord, bad as he might be, could not be worse than the slum landlord. The Land Acts found no counterpart in the shape of Town Acts to help workers to buy out their rooms in their tenements. These dispossessed descendants of dispossessed peasants had to get something. They began with wages. They ended up with rebellion. The docker, the tram-driver, the builder's labourer, the tradesmen were therefore the people who really began Irish revolutionary politics. The intellectuals, the artists, the poets, the writers, the liberals might be at the head of the procession; the houseless or wageless were the body of it. The Rising of 1916 was this typical amalgam, with Pearse, a poet schoolmaster, as its titular head and Connolly, the dockers' Union leader shoving behind so hard that the others had at one time to 'arrest' him in order to stop him from going out into bloody rebellion without them. But when it was all over the people who surged to the surface—pushing the intellectuals aside, as always happens in revolutions—were these children of the rotten quarter-acre of the 17th century demanding the thing for which they had fought, as their fathers had done before them in the fields: that is, cash, jobs, privileges and property. In a word they are demanding possession of the towns and cities as their fathers once demanded possession of the land.

If all this is far removed from our Connacht tenant-farmer of 1585, the first date at which we can identify him as holding a recognisable legal position in the social system; if Sir Richard Bingham had no idea that he was then creating what Euripides calls 'the men who alone save a nation'—and later upheavals were, in any case, so to persecute and depress the peasantry that their work in 'saving the nation' was to be political rather than social—the date is, nonetheless, a finger-post. Beyond it there rose, in time, this other finger-post showing the peasant, after many vicissitudes, entering into possession of a town-life which was made, in its beginnings, by Dane,

Norman, Tudor and Anglo-Irish. Here he now seems to be fumbling in an ungainly fashion with strange tools, rather lost, not very attractive, developing into a bastard type which is neither countryman nor townsman, unable, as yet, to make a smooth transition from the simplicity of the fields to the sophistication of the streets. In Ireland we call these men the new middle-classes or the new bourgeoisie, thinking of certain types that Balzac observed after another revolution. But we must postpone further consideration of them until we glance at a few of the later makers of the towns they grabbed.

The Anglo-Irish

THE LAST stand of the old Gaelic aristocracy, and its final defeat in the seventeenth century, has no more interest for us than the demolition of a house that has already been condemned. That last fight was conducted by a very great man indeed, Hugh O'Neill, Earl of Tyrone, and if anybody could have pulled the fractionalism of Ireland together he would have done it. But it is not necessary for us to delay over Tyrone's magnificent effort to save the Gaelic world from itself because we are already familiar with all its weaknesses. They merely appear the more exasperating at the end because Tyrone deserved better than to have to cope with them.

In my biography of Tyrone I have drawn all the usual conclusions, but one more occurs to me in this context. Tyrone had been reared as a child in England; he was one of the shrewdest men in the Europe of his day; he behaved all through his life as one who knows two worlds and can live at will in either; effectively, he was an Irish feudal baron of the greatest power, greater than any Norman baron had ever been, more powerful than Strongbow, or the Red Earl, or Ormond, or Desmond, any of whom, in England, would have been of the timber of kingmaker, and perhaps even of king. He could not have won in Ireland because his human material was not feudal. *Nobody* could have welded the Irish chiefs, except by hammering their proud heads together—and they would have returned joyously to their old ways immediately their dictator died.

The date of the defeat of Tyrone by Mountjoy, of his flight to the Continent, where he was received with the greatest honour and lodged in luxury in Rome by the Pope until his death, was 1603. That year is the great death-gong of Irish history, echoing back and back into the hollow halls of the Celtic world, mingling with the groans and sighs of a score of cursing kings who, like him, were thrown and trampled by the wild Irish mustangs. It echoes forward, for three hundred years, in tones of regret that grow ever softer and sweeter as the memory blurs until, by the end, one might almost think that this was Elysium and the Hesperides and Olympus and Arcadia all in one that the last poor, outcast Gaelic poetasters are for ever bewailing and eulogising: though, in truth, it *had* been an Arcadia for them—if for no one else. The new peasantry, whose arrival we have marked, were doubtless so foolish, at times, as to bewail it too.

How 'Partition' Began

Only one positive and creative thing came out of the last wreck of Gaeldom: Ulster as we now know it. O'Neill was an Ulster chief, and on his fall his territory was planted by English and Lowland Scots, mainly Presbyterian, but not wholly: the first Earl of Antrim was a Highlander and a Catholic. Many of the old Gaelic families remained on for a time in Ulster; few were to survive Cromwell. It was, as usual, only the small men who survived. They bowed to the storm; their standards were poor; they could be hired cheaply:

'It was not until after 1660 that the Scottish element in Ulster became a pronounced success and it is the only case of a real, democratic, industrial and labouring colony established in Ireland. Ulster finally became a province almost entirely Protestant as regards the landowners and mainly so as regards the population, and it is reckoned that in 1641 of the three and a half million acres in the Six Counties the Protestants owned three million and the Catholics the rest. But even this proportion was to be reduced after 1660, and after 1690 scarcely anything of the Gaelic and Catholic aristocracy remained.' *

This vast Plantation is the origin of Ireland's modern Partition problem; for interspersed with these colonists in the North-East a Catholic and Irish minority in the whole Province has tenaciously persisted to this day. The problem of Partition is primarily their problem. For the moment we may be content to observe this new, wholesale blending of fresh blood, this intrusion of another new mentality, and remember that still more plantations followed under James and Charles, in Wexford, Carlow and Wicklow, and there were wholesale clearances under Cromwell. So, in a county like Carlow one must expect to-day dominant twists of Gaelic and Norman, and seventeenth-century Protestant settlers, all now inextricably mingled with lesser healthy infusions unnoticed by any other histories than the parish records.

Nationalism Emerging

All through the seventeenth century, then, the old aristocratic Gaelic world was dying of the death-blow of 1603. It was in one sense a life-blow, a blow in the face that made the country awaken, though too late, far far

* Curtis: *History of Ireland,* p. 232.

too late, from its long somnambulism—or if not 'the
country' in any modern connotation, at any rate a greater
coherence of Irishmen than had ever been possible before.
Twice in the seventeenth century one can almost point, at
last, to a national mind—in the two great upheavals of the
Insurrection of 1641 and the Jacobite Wars that came to a
close with the Battle of the Boyne (1690) and the Siege
of Limerick (1691). Irishmen of every class and origin
took part in these wars, some fighting for religion, some
for land, some for Charles I or James II, some for the
old Gaelic traditional life-mode, some for an independent native parliament, some against this minor grievance,
some against that: and although we note that neither of
these wars was fought for what the modern vocabulary
would call 'Irish Independence'—and it was no longer
conceivable that any coherent fight could be raised for
any simple slogan—yet these wars of the seventeenth
century show one considerable development in Irish
thought: men were at last beginning to think in terms of
mutual accommodation, were learning that society is a
complex, and often a dissidence, and that there are techniques to bring this syncretism to a synthesis. Their tardy
efforts failed, but the experience cannot have been wholly
loss.

The Anglo-Irish

Out of this century in which the old aristocracy fell a
new aristocracy began to emerge. It was almost wholly
new, but not entirely so. True the 'old English,' mainly
Norman gentry, went down at the Boyne with the last
peerages of Gaelic blood—such as Iveagh and Clancarty.
But enough of these 'old English' remained to hand on

distinctively Irish ways and traditions to this Protestant and Anglican ascendancy that developed out of the plantations of James I and Cromwell. Bishop Berkeley (1685-1753), whose family had been only one generation in Ireland, could write at the close of his polemic against Newton: 'We Irish think otherwise'; and the two great Protestant defenders of Irish political rights in the eighteenth century, Swift and Molyneux, were sympathetic to many purely native traditions, the one praising the Catholic gentry defeated at the Boyne, the other taking a lively interest in the Gaelic language. This new ascendancy or aristocracy of the seventeenth century is what we call today 'the Anglo-Irish.' They were to bring to Ireland a greater concentration of civil gifts than any previous, or later, colonisers: one may, indeed, be done with it in one sentence by saying that culturally speaking the Anglo Irish were to create modern Ireland. Politically, and in the largest sense socially, they were either wicked, indifferent, or sheer failures.

The heyday of this Anglo-Irish enclave was the eighteenth century; their nearest-to-hand monument is Dublin's grace, roominess, magnificence and unique atmosphere; but all about the country they built gracious houses (each to be known to the native tenantry as 'The Big House') and pleasant seats, such as Castletown, near Dublin (1716) or Rockingham, near Boyle, County Roscommon (1810), which are the epitome of the classical spirit of that cultured and callous century. They were, however, a separate enclave. They resided in Ireland. It was their country, never their nation. So that their achievements were, for the most part, so remote from the life of the native Irish (now utterly suppressed) that they ultimately became part of the English rather than the Irish cultural

record. Swift, Goldsmith and Burke are obvious examples. But, as we may see in the next chapter, the Anglo-
Irish were far from being altogether an alien and de-
tached strain in Irish life. One need only mention such
names as Lord Edward Fitzgerald, or Robert Emmet, or
Thomas Davis, or Parnell to show at once that this is so.
One may see from the example of letters alone how active their interest was, how intimate and how fructive.
From the famous Protestant Archbishop James Ussher (*d.*
1656), or English Sir James Ware (*d.* 1666) to Charlotte
Brooke (*d.* 1793) or Charles Vallancey, an Englishman
of French Protestant parentage (*d.* 1812), the new ascendancy worked, in selfless devotion in generation after
generation, side by side with native Irishmen, to preserve
the traditions, language, and history of Ireland. These
men, and they were legion, were the forerunners of the
modern popular Gaelic Revival, whose founder (and
first President of Eire) was himself an Anglo-Irishman
of the Protestant faith.

Further Urbanisation

What the Normans had done was to bring the vigour of
their own, foreign, culture to bear on a decaying native
culture. Their gifts were social, political, and military.
As we have seen the chief thing they did was to urbanise
a pastoral people. The Anglo-Irish continued this urbanisation. All the planned aspects of the prettier villages
and towns in Ireland are their handiwork—Westport,
Lismore, Midleton, Youghal, Kinsale, the eighteenth-
century parts of Cork and Limerick, small villages like
Adare or Enniskerry, the quays of Clonmel, the pleasant
bits of Carlow and Kilkenny, Wexford and Birr: in every

Irish county they have left this welcome mark. I speak of it, however, not so much to indicate a further gift as to introduce the basic dichotomy. How often do we not meet on the edges of Irish towns, usually on the edge nearest the hinterland, a suburb known as 'Irishtown.' (See, for example, the Irishtown of Kilkenny, divided from the central town by a small—now concealed—river.) The barrier, that is to say, which originally existed between Normans and Gaels, and which was in the end worn away, was erected again by the Anglo-Irish, conveniently symbolised for us by these Irishtowns; or by those long, winding demesne walls which still so tiresomely blot out the scenery for the traveller.

The Religious Barrier

A new barrier, which was to prove the most formidable of all, was the difference in religion. The Normans were Catholics. The Anglo-Irish were Protestants or Anglicans. (Some of them are touchy about being called 'Non-Catholics' and Catholics so dislike the political connotations of Protestantism that, in mistaken delicacy, they think it milder to call them non-Catholics.) The outward symbol of that barrier is to find Catholic churches relegated to remote or back streets (cheaper ground, also less likely to attract attention) and Protestant churches plumb in the middle of a town square, or on the hill: and one will note how often the Catholic church is without a spire— that little arrogance was forbidden by law. Thus in my native city of Cork the great trident of the spires of the Protestant Cathedral dominate the city, all the older Catholic churches are hidden away, and none has a spire. These things remind us that one of the most cultivated and creative societies in western Europe during the eighteenth century was also politically barbarous.

And now for the solution of this dichotomy. The century was not without a conscience—noble-minded men who loathed the injustices they saw about them on all sides, and in the Dublin Parliament, now a real capital and the final centre of the island's life, strained to alleviate them. These were the 'Patriot Party' reviving the old Norman claims to autonomy in terms of a new Protestant nationalism. They fought local corruption, British interference, demanded Free Trade, control of revenue, sought to relieve the Catholic masses from the worst of their local disabilities, but, on the other hand, had no idea of any organic change in the social system that kept these masses of tenantry in a condition so beastly that Chesterfield thought them treated worse than Negro slaves.

Anglo-Irish Patriotism

The Patriot Party gave the native Irish some alleviations but their real gift was a great political lesson which was to dominate the popular imagination for the next hundred and forty years. They seized on the foreign troubles of England, in America, France, Spain, and Holland, to found an armed force of Protestant Volunteers, originally and ostensibly to defend the country against invasion, ultimately and ostentatiously to win the absolute independence of the Irish Parliament; which they did in 1782. True, this bloodless revolt proved abortive; firstly, because the Parliament represented only the Anglo-Irish enclave, and could not gather up enough vision or courage to give the vote to the Roman Catholic

majority, and secondly, because in 1800, two years after
the native Irish, at last driven to desperation, has risen
in rebellion, the Dublin Parliament was completely
abolished by Pitt. But the memory of the Volunteers
never died, and gave to the masses the famous motto
that 'England's difficulty is Ireland's opportunity,' with
its implied reliance on physical force and its evident de-
spair of all constitutional techniques. Above all, as we
must next see by going back a few years to 1791, this
armed defiance of the Patriot Party created a new Irish
type, the Rebel, in whom native Irish and Anglo-Irish
became and have ever since found the personification of
a single-minded nationalism.

Before leaving the Protestant, settler, landowning
Anglo-Irish we must add that while these intrusives became the dominant aristocracy of the country—thanks to
wealth, position and the approval of the Government
of the country of their origin—and that, while things were
thus simply arranged as a division of depressed native
and prosperous settler, there did remain a scattered midway class of better-off native Irish. These would be Catholic (though keeping rather quiet about it), comfortable,
and in politics strictly constitutional—in so far as they
ventured to think of such matters at all. Some of them
were in trade in the cities. Some farmed. Some liked to
think of themselves as gentlemen. Some were proud of
their descent from the now vanished native aristocracy
—kings and chiefs and heads of 'clans.' This midway class
of men were not fated to make any great mark on the
life of their country—its problems were too harsh and
had to be handled in too crude, and indeed bloody, a way
for them to find any effective role in it. Yet they must be
mentioned lest the picture appear over-simplified into

a cartoon of lords and slaves, true though that cartoon is in general outline.

In fact they have to be mentioned just because the cartoon became all too true, and to explain why it did. They answer, that is to say, a question which may naturally occur to the outsider:—'Where was the native leadership?' It was by 1750 dim and timid and, to be rather brutal about it, tended, not unnaturally to become 'respectable,' and aloof. The Catholic native gentleman was in the main, like the Catholic Scottish gentleman, a virtual recluse. An average example from the late 18th and early 19th century would be the O'Conor Don, at one time Editor of *The Freeman's Journal*, residing in Connacht, proud to the last degree of his descent from native royalty, amiable, intelligent, estimable; willing to co-operate with Catholic gentlemen like Lord Fingall for the alleviation of oppressive laws on Catholics; willing to co-operate even with that rude and powerful demagogue and ultimate Emancipator of his race, Daniel O'Connell, as long as everything was done constitutionally and in order; named as a Lord of the Treasury; and finally dropping out of the game as it falls into the hands of ruder and more ruthless men. The whole of the history of the constitutional movement of the 19th century is full of the names of such men of the middle class, mostly now forgotten; for, ironically, those better known were of the clear-cut Protestant Anglo-Irish tradition—Mitchel, Tone, Davis or Parnell are cases in point. And to one of these we must now turn in the track of history.

The Rebels

In 1791, in Belfast, that house built upon a house, among the Presbyterian Dissenters, there was founded a secret society known as The United Irishmen aiming at a 'brotherhood of affection and a communion of rights and a union of power among Irishmen of every religious persuasion.' The source of this generative idea was France. I have earlier quoted W. P. Ker on the old Celtic mind and its literature to intimate that its struggle was towards intellectual and imaginative freedom. We have seen in that literature one or two abortive adventures of the racial kind groping for this freedom. It is striking that, in the end, it is not in culture but in politics, not in Gaelic Ireland but in Anglo-Ireland, not among Catholics but Nonconformists that the fog suddenly lifts on a bit of clear-cut logic. But no word must be said that would suggest for a moment a cold or abstract mind. The chief figure of the United Irishmen was a man of charming personality, merry wit, and civilised ideas about life in general. He had had noble precursors and contemporaries—Swift is an example of the one and Grattan of the other—but, to steal the words of a famous password about another amiable Irishman, 'Wolfe Tone is the name and Wolfe Tone is the man.' This young Protestant Dubliner, educated at Trinity College, that alien nursery of native causes, was to unite the logic of the Northern Scot to the passions of the Southern Irish, to scatter the timidities of the peasants and the vacillations of the tradesmen and native gentlemen with his vision of the new revolutionary age. In Tone's hands the French Revolution became a trumpet, unheard indeed by the dust of antiquity, and one can only laugh to think what the bardic caste would have said of him; heard by only a small number of the millions of slaves about him, but heard by enough men to have handed down to our day, a gay and passionate republican spirit that is never likely to die wholly in Ireland.

Irish Jacobinism

The cleavage with the past is immense. A century before and the fumes of a thousand years were still lingering about us. Almost without warning Wolfe Tone flings open the doors of the modern world like a thunder-clap. Nothing less dramatic can describe a change so great as to see Jacobin ideas spreading, at whatever highly simplified remove from their original form, among a Gaelic-speaking peasantry.

This combination of what one must call a controlled Anglo-Irish intelligence and a passionate sense of injustice among the native Irish—in so far as there was by now any blood unmixed enough to be called 'native Irish'—is the formula of modern Irish nationalism. Tone, Parnell and Griffith are examples. The common people burned with a sense of their undeniable wrongs; the new middle-classes, of whatever religion, found their country—or the country of their adoption—being misruled by an utterly corrupt, inefficient and pandering Parliament in the selfish interests of Britain. But the peasantry had no ideas

and the middle-classes had no force. The peasantry did, indeed, form into secret violent societies (The White-boys and Shanavests and so forth) to revenge themselves on local tyrants; and for the enlargement or sublimation of their hates and hopes could still listen to the wandering Gaelic poets weaving Vision Poems, or *Aislingi,* in which the ancient world was once again restored by the Stuarts returning in triumph from France or Spain. But neither these impossible dreams nor those sporadic outbursts could be of much help, except as a heady drink may keep up a poor devil's spirits until his real chance arrives. Neither could the timid methods of the Catholic Whiggish middle-classes achieve much by loyal addresses since they were content to accept the current social order provided they could remove the restrictions under which their own class suffered: they were otherwise indifferent to the real canker of their country, i.e. the hideous economic slavery in which the masses of the people existed as mere cottiers without rights, without security, without a vote, without hope. It was from the top alone, from the free-minded intellectuals, such as Tone, and from the more humane aristocrats of the new Anglo-Irish order that a fighting leadership could come. Since, in the end, the aristocracy was subject to the corruption of its own vested interests, which not even the devotion of Grattan and his 'Patriot Party' could hold at bay, that leadership of the people devolved in the end on the intellectuals.*
They became the interpreters of the new America and

* It was not, in fact, until Tone and his comrades expelled the tame Catholic aristocrats from their committees that they won, by the Relief Act of 1793, the removal of the major disabilities under which Catholics had suffered since Limerick and the Boyne, e.g., they could carry a gun, go to Dublin University (Protestant—the only University), vote as forty-shilling freeholders in the counties, hold minor offices, act as grand jurors, take commissions in the army.

the new France. Thanks to their propaganda the vacuum
left in the Irish mind by the fall of the Norman and Gaelic
aristocracy was filled by the most explosive ideas of modern democratic Europe.

Things have so much changed since that century, there
are now so many other quarters from which leadership
might at any moment emerge for a national agitation—
the Church, the writers, the Labour movement, our political parties, the Press—that we must emphasise this isolation of Tone and his companions in the Ireland of the
1790's. I have mentioned five modern alternatives; obviously the last four did not then exist. We must see, too,
why the Catholic Church was to all intents and purposes
wholly supine at this period.

A Supine Church

It was not until the first decade of the following century
that any signs of spirit appear among the Catholic clergy,
and then a man like the famous 'J. K. L.,' James Warren
Doyle, Bishop of Kildare and Leighlin, forms an astonishing contrast not only to his predecessors but even to his
contemporaries. This is not surprising. We remember
that for generations the official—and legal—title for a
Catholic was 'Papist'; that the Catholic Church was never
referred to as such but as 'the Roman Catholic communion
in Ireland,' as if it were a peculiar local sect; that priests
generally dressed in discreet brown so as not to attract
attention; are always (as in Tone's diaries) spoken of as
'Mister' So-and-so; that an Archbishop of Dublin, in for-
warding a curate's letter to Dublin Castle for perusal,
could add, 'You note he calls me "Lord," but I do not
claim the title, and I can't prevent him from using it';

that, as Tom Moore noted in his Diary, whereas Archbishop Troy, the Catholic, died worth tenpence the Protestant Archbishop of Armagh left £130,000, having throughout his life enjoyed an income of £20,000 a year, largely made up of the pence of peasants (Catholics) unwillingly subscribed as tithes. It sums up the dispiritedness of the Catholic Church that when Dr. Doyle became Bishop—Tone then seventeen years dead—he found that nobody had dared hold a confirmation service in his diocese for twenty years, his chapels were thatched cabins, the vestments were worn and torn, the chalices were old or even leaked.

'J. K. L.' did, in his day, give magnificent encouragement to his people. On the other hand he was a rigid constitutionalist: his great opponents were the secret societies that the rebelly spirit of the century before had set flourishing among the tough men of the collieries, and he fought them to his dying day—often literally with the sweat pouring off him, haranguing them in their basalt thousands under the open sky. This horror of physical revolt, of all revolutionary defiance for established law and order, goes so deep into the spirit of the Church of the time that it is worth probing a little further into the causes of it, and its prolonged effects.

Catholic Loyalists

As we know, the great Catholic seminary of Maynooth was founded, long before Catholic Emancipation, even before the '98 Rebellion, out of British Government funds. We need not enquire whether the Government hoped to purchase the loyalty of the Church; for though it certainly got it, that was because of chance circumstances

that it could not have foreseen. In 1795, the year of Maynooth's foundation, there were a great many French refu-
gee professors and teachers to whom any haven, the most
frugal pension, would have been welcome. This suited
Maynooth perfectly, for it was not a rich foundation, and,
as one may imagine, Ireland (just emerging from the
Penal Code) was in no position to supply it with sufficient native scholars. It gave posts to several of these distinguished men, such as Delahogue and Anglade for
moral and dogmatic theology, thereby importing a
French school of thought whose teachings so carefully,
indeed fanatically, cultivated the spirit of Gallicanism
among the Irish clergy that the Irish Church soon became
Gallican to the core, and remained so for nearly half a
century. That is: in politics, through their hatred of the
Revolutionary spirit, in their devotion to the old mon-
archical absolutism, they filled the mind of most Irish
priests, all through O'Connell's great fight against Britain,
with the traditional Gallican belief that all things, even
many of the privileges of the Church, must lie in servile
subjection to the throne; and, in morals, they encouraged
a repulsive rigour in the management of consciences
which rendered the following of Christ's teachings anything but a *jugum suave*. They proscribed many of the
classic theologians of the Church, such as Suarez or Mo-
lina, both Jesuits, the first of whom had written against
the Oath of Allegiance to the crown, the second of whom
had humanely tried to reconcile free will and predestina-
tion. Liguori, even after his beatification, was not safe
from the censure of those bitter French exclusivists at
Maynooth—one actually told his students that the saint
was *perditè laxus*. They were so far from all accommoda-
tiveness, benignity, mildness, so far from trying to make

the Law easier for the people, that one of the prevailing class-books at Maynooth, that of Bailly, had to be put on the Index in 1852. 'An alien theology possessing for us neither national nor other interest thus balefully affected the youth and manhood of the Irish Church, narrowing their views, misdirecting their professional studies and if not entirely estranging their feelings of allegiance at least sensibly weakening them towards the true object of Catholic loyalty.'

When this mentality was finally exorcised from May-nooth I do not know; it cannot have outlasted the 1850's but it had by then been carried through the length and breadth of Ireland by priests educated under the old ré-gime, and when a sharp controversy (from which I take the last quotation) developed in 1879 over a sudden lift-ing of the veil by Dr. Henry Neville, Rector of the Catholic University, ex-professor of Maynooth, one of the reasons why his would-be refuter (Dr. Walsh, later Archbishop Walsh; died 1921), was angry with him was that so many priests who had passed through the College in the epoch under question were still working among the people. One feels that a tradition like that eddies on. Even in our day readers of Canon Sheehan's excellent novel, *The Blindness of Doctor Gray,* will recognise a familiar priest of the old school, the stern moralist for whom 'The Law' was a second god. One meets its eddies constantly in the political and clerical history of the nineteenth century, as in 'J. K. L.'s' disagreements with Delahogue and Anglade (see Fitzpatrick's *Life,* pages 83, 156), MacHale's with O'Finan (O'Reilly's *Life,* I, 345), or again in Doyle's brush with the Jesuits at Clongowes (*op. cit.,* p. 142) whom he tried to *stop* from hearing confessions because he thought them too lenient! And, of course, as we know, both Doyle and MacHale were anti-French because of their youthful experiences, the latter in Ireland, the former in Portugal when Napoleon invaded it in 1807 (he stood sentry at Coimbra during those exciting months, and went to Lisbon to act as interpreter for the English under that other famous Irishman, Wellesley). But if one grasps this key one understands a lot of things much better, especially why it was that O'Connell had to fight not merely the British but his own bishops, the English and Irish Catholic aristocrats, and even defy Rome herself in the famous Veto question, i.e. the 'right' of the Crown to hand-pick Ireland's Bishops, as Grattan weakly offered—that being the occasion of O'Connell's famous *pronunciamento* that if the Catholics of Ireland must accept the order of Pius VII to accept royal nomination of their own bishops he would, in future, rather take his politics from Constantinople than from Rome, and that such bishops would, in fact, be the means of uncatholicising the land.* One understands best of all what a task poor Tone had, away back in the 1790's, to rouse the Catholic laity and priesthood.

Wolfe Tone Alone

The masses, then, had no other fighting leaders but Tone and The United Irishmen in the 1790's; and these were trying to build up a new mentality, a new mind, against every opposition. Of that new mind Tone, first and before all others, is the personification. That was

---

* It sums up the period, 1805 to 1845, to say that O'Connellism in the presbytery was fighting, and defeating, Gallicanism in the seminary. Long before O'Connell there were, of course, noble exceptions among the priesthood: one has only to recall the priests who died with the gun in their hands in '98, or who were hanged or shot after the Rising ended.

his main contribution, to give to his people the dynamism of his own nature, the example of his own life. Overtly he and The United Irishmen were to achieve, directly or indirectly, very little: the bloody Rising of '98, a failure; two abortive efforts to invade Ireland from France; a brief rising in the West. But he was to sow ideas broadcast. He was to present common men with their first personal hero of the new democratic age. He was to leave behind him a diary in which his merry, insuppressible, eager, all too human nature, so sceptical, so serious, so gay, so indiscreet, so utterly removed from all posing or false dignity, is a happy definition not merely of the man but of his ideals. It and he are the only sensible definition that exists of what Irishmen mean to-day when they talk of being Republicans. He was to become the beau-ideal of Irish rebels, the great prototype on which all later would-be revolutionaries instinctively modelled themselves.

This rebel mentality has become so rooted in Ireland and has so coloured all our other characteristics, and so profoundly affected our social behaviour, our symbolism, our literature, even our conventions, that we should strive hard to understand it. Irishmen themselves possibly understand it least of all since with them it is not so much a question of understanding as of the dissection of something too familiar even to propose self-questions.

The Rebel as a Type

The rebel seems to fall into two types or stages. The one rebels against an immediate injustice—peasant risings follow, peasant societies of revenge, workers' associations. He sees no further. The other sees beyond the immediate thing to the larger implications: he is the man who uses words like Emancipation, Liberty, Freedom. The one is clear as to his object; the other is never clear. He cannot be because his desirable image of life is not something which forms in a vacuum but something whose instruments are flesh and blood. He is subject to the limitations of his followers and times. This intellectual type of rebel is always the national leader, as against the local leader, and it is his dilemma that, in the ultimate, he is leading people to a Promised Land which *they*, not he, must define and create. He is riding a raft on a swirling river, and like all leaders of masses of men it may well be his constant problem whether he is riding the torrent or the torrent is driving him.

The Rebel probably never cared. He was devoted to failure. He was a professional or vocational failure. Not that he did not dream of and hope for success. But he always knew the odds were against him and if he was a Wolfe Tone, laughed cheerfully at his possible, indeed probable, fate. (Tone joked over the usual fate of his kind—to be hanged and disembowelled. 'A fig for the disembowelling if they hang me first.') There was only one thing at which the Rebel wished to be a success and that was at rebelling. Death did not mean failure so long as the Spirit of Revolt lived. The Rebel did not even mind obliteration and anonymity, and thousands upon thousands of Irish rebels have never been recorded and their sacrifice will never be known.

Rebel Idealism

Nor are Irish rebels peculiar in this. One of the most eloquent tributes ever paid to anonymous sacrifice occurs in that remarkable, and too little known, English novel, *The Revolution in Tanner's Lane,* by Mark Rutherford. I think it worth giving here in full:

'To work hard for those who will thank us, to head a majority against oppressors is a brave thing; but far more honour is due to (those) who strove for thirty years from the outbreak of the French Revolution onwards not merely to rend the chains of the prisoners, but had to achieve the far more difficult task of convincing them that they would be happier if they were free. These heroes are forgotten or nearly so. Who remembers the poor creatures who met in the early mornings on the Lancashire moors or were shot by the yeomanry? They sleep in graves over which stands no tombstone, or probably their bodies have been carted away to make room for a railway which has been driven through their last resting-place. They saw the truth before those whom the world delights to honour as its political redeemers; but they have perished utterly from our recollection and will never be mentioned in history. Will there ever be a great Day of Assize when a just judgement shall be pronounced; when all the impostors who have been crowned for what they did not deserve will be stripped, and the Divine word will be heard calling upon the faithful to inherit the Kingdom,—who, when "I was an hungered gave me meat, when I was thirsty gave me drink; when I was a stranger took me in; when I was naked clothed me; when I was in prison came unto me"? Never! It was a dream of an enthusiastic Galilean youth, and let us not desire that it may ever come true. Let us rather gladly consent to be crushed into indistinguishable dust, with no hope of record: rejoicing only if some infinitesimal portion of the good work may be achieved by our obliteration, and content to be remembered only in that anthem which in the future it will be ordained shall be sung in our religious services in honour of all holy apostles and martyrs who have left no name.'

Rebel Tolerance

Even of those who are recorded, honoured and well known what *is* known clearly? The one thing about them which is always clear is their personalities. Thus, what Tone would have done had he been first President of an Irish Republic nobody knows, because he has not told us. But from the nature of the man we can see the kind of life that would have pleased him, and the things (for example) in this modern Ireland that he would not have tolerated, such as the least sign of sectarianism, puritanism, middle-class vulgarity, canting pietism, narrow orthodoxies whether of Church or State. One feels that his laughter and his humanity would have blown all these away, would have defined political liberty not merely in terms of comfort but of gaiety and tolerance and a great pity and a free mind and a free heart and a full life. And if few rebels have been so gay as Tone, except perhaps in our own time Mick Collins, wherever the Rebel appears he will always reveal the same composition—even the most solemn and subjective of them, such as Pearse—or else he is a faux-rebel or a lapsed-rebel, that most common and pathetic type in the history of all peoples.

The thing could not have· been otherwise. Rebelly Wolfe Tone was doomed to leave so little behind him, to be unclear in his ideas, to be fuddled even, to be a failure, because he chose to lock-knit himself with the common people, with the poorest and most ignorant of his country· men whose whole lives, day after day, were themselves the very epitome of befuddlement and failure. He was not their tutor: he was their torch, their friend, their lover. He went down into the huts and cabins and took the people to his heart. He was not telling them about their future—they had no future. He was telling them about their present—about themselves. He was their second priest. It was rebels like him whom in turn the poor have always loved with an unbreakable loyalty, made ballads about them, hung their likenesses in cheap pictures about their walls, revered as their symbols— Tone, Emmet, Lord Edward, Napper Tandy, O'Connell, Mitchel, Parnell and all the rebels of 1916 and after.

This is not to detract from those other Irishmen of the midway class, mentioned at the close of the chapter on the Anglo-Irish, who, in their humanity, kindness and sensibility, contributed throughout the nineteenth century to the spirit of liberalism, but who pledged their minds to success in the sense that as gradualists they were satisfied to win reform little by little, and to clearsightedness in the sense that they would not look beyond those immediate and possible goals. These were our pure constitutionalists like that devoted and patriotic first leader of the Irish Party, Isaac Butt, and its last leader John Redmond, and there were earlier men, like John Keogh, and hundreds of others earlier and later still, and doubtless there always will be, whose natural sense of decencies ranges them, though at a remove of prudence or qualified disapproval, on the side of (if not beside) the rebelly-minded.

A good example of these men was O'Connell's lieutenant O'Neill Daunt whose autobiography, well-named *A Life Spent for Ireland,* loyally veils but does not conceal his distaste for O'Connell's techniques. But just as it is quite evident that O'Neill Daunt could never have accomplished what O'Connell accomplished by his rumbustuous, indeed often, if not always, slightly vulgar, flamboyant defiance, his—call it if one wills tricky or even dishonest—methods of inflaming the people to the very edge of open revolt, and as in the Tithe War well beyond it, in short by his use of the rebel-mind in thought and action, so never once, I dare say, did any constitutionalist win one of those gradual reforms without the Rebel as the real force behind him.

The Rebel Tradition

This is illustrated over and over during the hundred years after Tone. It is that century in a nutshell. Tone died in 1798. O'Connell was at work from 1807. The next rebel movement, the Young Irelanders, began in 1842 and broke into armed revolt on his death. Ten years later Fenianism began under Stephens and O'Donovan Rossa, and there were attempted outbreaks in '65 and '67. That 'life and death question' of Ireland in the nineteenth century, Land trouble—which had scattered violence all over the country ever since O'Connell's day with its inevitable aftermaths of evictions and emigrations—was boiling ever since 1852, and was to be the centre of the Parnellite campaign. Interwoven with all this was the constitutional effort. Isaac Butt, to lead the Irish Party from 1870 on, defended the Fenians in '65. Parnell was converted to Nationalism by the execution of the three Irish Fenians who attempted the famous prison release in Manchester in 1867. The first of a series of Land Acts that were, ultimately, to change the whole character of the peasantry, namely Gladstone's Act of 1870, came out of violence and murder in Tipperary. The Land Bill of 1881, which at last fixed the tenant's rent and prevented landlords from practising any longer that brutal and ambition-destroying trick of increasing the rent whenever a tenant by his own industry improved his holding, came out of one of the most violent periods of Davitt's Land League agitation. And so on.

If there is in all this a distinction between the 'common people' and others who are not 'the people' I can only say *Circumspice*. That is the way the story has gone. I say it in no spirit of democratic enthusiasm for the 'common people' who are, to the artist and the intellectual, so often a bore and an aggravation, whose lives and minds are most creative and interesting when they themselves are most poor and least emancipated, as when Yeats 'discovered' them, still a traditional peasantry.

Rebel Sacrifice

What was it that the Irish Rebel always sacrificed? The better part of his life? Far worse, far more exhausting, harder far to bear, he sacrificed the better part of his mind. Men like Tone, Mitchel, Doheny, all of them, had smothered talents. They were presumably men with as much human ambition as anybody else, and more sensibility than most. It was a drudge to them to 'go down into the cabins of the people.' How bored Tone was by these talks and meals with dithering, half-educated, Catholic tradesmen and farmers; and he was the last man to whine or complain. 'Cowardly enough.' 'A dirty personal jealousy.' 'Our mob, very shabby fellows.' 'Shabby.' 'A blockhead, without parts or principles.' 'The parish priest, a sad vulgar booby.' 'Egan of Galway is flinching.' 'Sick.' 'Victuals bad, wine poisonous, bed execrable.' 'Sad, sad.' 'Dinner with the Catholics, dull as ten thousand devils. Dismal, dreary.' 'Damn them, ignorant bigots' (this about two Catholic bishops) . 'Gog (this is John Keogh, the most pious of Catholics and most devoted, though timid) tells me he begins to see the Catholic bishops are all scoundrels.' 'Cowardly! Cowardly!' (this about men who are trying to dodge taking the chair at a meeting) . And so it goes on. But how even that far tougher metal, the great and burly Dan O'Connell, used to curse those 'common people' as when he called them 'animals,' and 'crawling slaves!'

Emotion or Thought?

All these men deprived Ireland of as much as they gave to it: they choked the critical side of their minds, they were good rebels in proportion as they were bad revolutionaries, so that their passion for change and their vision of change never pierced to organic change, halted dead at the purely modal and circumstantial. It had to be that way since they devoted their lives and all their beings to passion rather than to thought, or in Arnold's words describing the French Revolution 'had their source in a great movement of feeling, not in a great movement of mind.' Not that Arnold's ideas in the first of his *Essays in Criticism* have any political validity, and certainly no validity as between Ireland and England since (as he recognises freely, certainly by implication throughout) you might as well try to change an Englishman's political views about his Empire by reasoning with him as hope to stop the charge of an elephant with an epigram. And, furthermore, as Arnold also agrees, though so subtly as to gloss over the inherent contradiction, the French Revolution

'undoubtedly found its motive-power in the intelligence of
men . . . The French Revolution derives from the force,
truth and universality of the ideas which it took for its law,
and from the passion with which it could inspire these
ideas, a unique and still living power; it is—it will probably long remain—the greatest, the most animating event
in history. And as no sincere passion for the things of the
mind, even though it turn out in many respects an unfortu-
nate passion, is ever quite thrown away and quite barren of
good, France has reaped from hers one fruit—the natural
and legitimate fruit, though not precisely the grand fruit
she expected; she is the country in Europe where *the people* is most alive.'

Yet, it is for all that still true of our Irish rebels that it
was upon the emotional content of the Revolution that
they seized and not on its intellectual content, with the
result that the whole of Irish patriotic literature ever
since has either concerned itself with matters of sentiment
rather than thought; or with interim solutions of immediate problems that time has since dealt with otherwise.
Irish political thought is thus, to this day, in its infancy. In
other words if, as I said in discussing The New Peasantry,
the countryman who has invaded the towns is now fumbling there in an ungainly fashion it is because his intellectual leaders were so damnably un-intellectual. We
Irish have run all our rebellions on our emotions, and we
are now paying for the luxury. As an idea Republicanism
in Ireland aborted. It created a type and popularised a
spirit. The Irishman the world over is to this day a noncon-
formist and a rebel—it is one of his great gifts to an over-
regimented world; but the rebel gave nothing to political
science—gave less even than the priest was to give to the
science of religion. Always we seem to be excellent at the
thing, but not good at the idea.

The Priests

ALTHOUGH CHRISTIANITY came to Ireland in the fifth century the Catholic priest, without whom any picture of modern Ireland is unthinkable, does not occupy a central position in that picture until the nineteenth century. The distinction is a political one, for it has to be accepted that what has given the Catholic clergy their social prominence to-day is their political influence, and that without that influence the priest would no more take the centre of the stage in Irish life than does the parson in English life. When the priest did not possess this political influence he was, indeed, in his own religious realm, adored, feared and obeyed; one could nevertheless describe whole centuries without one personal reference to the robe—no matter how often one considered it necessary to keep on insisting that the people were devotedly Catholic. See, for example, the fourteenth and fifteenth centuries.

What I mean by political influence had better be defined at once. I mean, quite simply, influence in the political arena. I do not mean that the priest exercises this influence for the mere sake of power; or that he is not fully entitled to this influence; or that he always employs this influence which he possesses; or, using the word 'priest' as a personification of the Church, that he ever exercises this influence for the mere purposes of party politics; nor, indeed, do I think that he has any interest in these matters at all except where they concern religion; though what concerns religion is, of course, the debatable point. An Early Closing Act is hardly likely to concern religion. The early or late closing of taverns may or may not. The closing or opening of brothels does. Nevertheless, in *all* of these matters the priest can exercise a great influence in the political arena. Until that power came his way he was not the prominent figure in Irish life that he is to-day.

Slow Rise to Power

Throughout the earlier centuries the priest was never a prominent figure. The prominent figures, then, were monks. That was because monasticism was the focus of early Irish Christianity, and even after the Norman Reformation has changed that by establishing an episcopal organisation, it is the abbot and the abbey which still attract most attention until the Elizabethan age. Then, for the first time, the priest begins to exercise a political influence, though not so much the seculars as the orders. The 'Friar' is the most adored as the Jesuit is the most admired figure of the sixteenth century. (The word 'adored' is taken from the report of Capuys, the imperial ambassador in London, writing about Ireland to Charles V in 1534, and he also uses the words 'obeyed' and 'feared.')

These influential figures were not always Irishmen. The outstanding religious figures of the sixteenth-century 'Holy War' of James Fitzmaurice were Oviedo, a Spanish Franciscan, and Dr. Nicholas Sanders, an English Jesuit. The great clerical figure of the seventeenth-century Confederate Wars was the Italian Archbishop of Fermo, John

Baptist Rinuccini. But the brunt of the work of the
Counter-Reformation was done by Irish priests. Two of
the earliest martyrs were Bishop O'Healy of Mayo, and
his comrade Father O'Rourke who landed in Dingle a
short while before James Fitzmaurice and Sanders spread
in the winds of Kerry the papal standard they brought
with them from Rome. The most notable victim of the
period was the papal Archbishop of Cashel, Dermot
O'Hurley, tortured and executed in Dublin in 1584.
Under James I this persecution of Catholicism began to
make the priest a personification of that powerful combination of political and religious resistance to English
rule which was, for a time, to become basic in Irish nationalism. The recipe was established by Cromwell under
whom—it should be enough, at this day, to recall but one
horribly picturesque item from many cruel edicts—it became law that any man who wanted to earn £5 need but
produce the head of a wolf or of a priest, it did not matter which.

The eighteenth century elevated the priest spiritually
in proportion as it debased him socially. He became the
only intelligent companion the people had, excepting
only the travelling Gaelic poets. But, both priest and
poet were now weak *political* reeds. Right up to the
union of Britain and Ireland in 1800, the terminus of the
century, the constant policy of the hierarchy was to proclaim its loyalty to the Throne in the hope of winning at
least some reliefs from the Penal Laws. Thus, the Catholic bishops, like the Catholic aristocrats, were in favour
of the Union of Great Britain and Ireland—being grossly
deceived by Pitt into believing that Catholic Relief
would follow. The coldly disapproving attitude of the
clergy to rebellion, let alone disloyalty, fostered by the

Gallicanism of Maynooth, persisted into the nineteenth century; long after the death of the man who finally made the priest a representative national figure—that great demagogue and organiser of Catholic resistance, Dan O'Connell.

The dates of his life-work are from about 1805 to 1845. In those forty years O'Connellism gradually undermined the conservatism of Maynooth. After all, the priests might understandably draw back from Tone's doctrines of French Republicanism and Irish armed resistance: they could hardly hold back from O'Connell's constitutional fight for Catholic Emancipation, or his later fight against Tithes. Not that they flocked at once to O'Connell's side. On the contrary, his letters give many indications of popular resentment against them for their inaction at the start of his fight, especially on the question of the Government's claim to handpick Catholic bishops, to which the entire Board of Maynooth at one time agreed and on which some of the most influential bishops, such as the Archbishop of Dublin, constantly wobbled. ('There is a tendency already to substitute friars for any priests who are supposed to favour the Veto.' Or, again:

'You cannot conceive anything more lively than the abhorrence of the Vetoistical plans among the people at large. I really think they will go near to desert all such clergymen as do not now take an active part on the question. The Methodists were never in so fair a way of making converts.')

Gradually he rallied the mass of the priests behind him. Once in the arena they fought manfully. Before he died he was to find that he was behind them. Inevitably and properly, they had kept their autonomy; until at the close of his career, he found himself being dictated to by the bishops—on the controversial question of popular and higher education, the National Schools and the University question.

The Priest in Politics

By 1850, then, that terrible bogy-man of the nineteenth century all over Europe, the 'Priest in Politics,' has arrived in Ireland. In other words, the priest in a country about ninety per cent. Catholic is the barometer of the political emancipation of the majority. His rise followed their rise. By 1850 the Catholic Church in Ireland had a well-established seminary. It was not a wealthy foundation. The original grant, of 1795, was a mere £8,000, which the Government did not increase until 1807 and then, in the face of a bigoted opposition, only to something under £10,000. Why there should have been such opposition is now hard to understand since Maynooth was loyal beyond suspicion: ever since the day of its foundation it had been strictly enjoined by Propaganda at Rome to give an example of unswerving loyalty to the Crown 'at all times and places.' A frank history of that struggling Maynooth would make moving reading: the internal tensions between Irishmen and foreigners, the insistent poverty, the naïveties and crudities of the poor peasant students who must often have worn the patience of their teachers—at least once there were student riots behind which one can feel the patriotic passions of peasant Ireland breaking through the French rigorism of the seminary. Things did ease a little in 1845 when the grant rose to £23,360, with £30,000 for buildings: but a bitter price had to be paid for this Government assistance—lack of

freedom, lay visitations, discussions in Parliament, en-
quiries by Government Commissions: one may imagine
how any Oxford college would have loathed that sort of
thing from its own government, not to speak of a foreign
government. When the grant was commuted for a capital
sum in 1869, at the time of Church Disestablishment, and
these inspections and controls were removed, Maynooth
could straighten its back, although now poorer by half.
The bishops had £369,000 on hand, buildings and lands,
somewhere around £15,000 for annual burses, and students' fees: the whole of which, invested, would not bring
in half of the former grant. (The Disestablished Church
was, at the same date, receiving about eight million pounds
in capital values.)

The priest was now completely free, and established in
his freedom. Persecution was gone for ever; his was a recognised profession; he had an enormous local personal
influence; his flock had the franchise and they were the
majority of the population. This man, who had once been
hunted like a wild beast, then barely tolerated, then grudg-
ingly acknowledged as a citizen, was now a power that
no local or national politician could ignore.

In Literature .

From very soon after Emancipation the priest begins
to enter contemporary fiction—in Carleton, Lever, Lover
and others—and one may see him in general outline as he
struck observers, prejudiced and otherwise. He rarely
comes from the middle-classes, he is farmer-stock, often
put through college at a great sacrifice by poor parents;
he is not very cultivated, he has not been cut off from the
people by his education, they feel him as one of them-

selves. (In passing, at least some contemporary politicians
felt that when Peel proposed a University for the Catholics and increased the Maynooth grant he had in mind
the hope of attracting priests from a higher class, and of
cultivating them away from the peasantry.) All these novelists agree on the priest's great influence in local politics: their characterisations imply various explanations
for it. One of the earliest novels dealing with priests sym-
pathetically is Banim's *Father Connell* (1840). I find it
rather sentimental. Others have approved of it wholeheartedly.

'The character is one of the noblest in fiction. He is the
ideal Irish priest, almost childlike in simplicity, pious, lav-
ishly charitable, meek and long-suffering but terrible when
circumstances roused him to action.' *

There the priest's influence is moral. At the other end
of the scale is *Misther O'Ryan* by Edward M'Nulty (1894)
in which the priest is an ugly, whisky-drinking, vulgar
fellow. His influence is that of a bully and a political
intriguer. In both of these books one may confidently
perceive not objectively observed human beings but per-
sonifications of the same political sympathies and prejudices that one sometimes finds in Balzac's novels.

Most writers, if they do not follow those extreme lines,
see the priest in one of three aspects—the jovial, hunting,
hearty priest, who is really a 'good fellow' in clerical
garb; or the rigorous, unbending, saintly and generally
rather inhuman ascetic—the patriarch of his flock; or
the man whose life is one long psychological problem. In
one or other of these aspects he has been drawn over and

* *A Reader's Guide to Irish Fiction.* Rev. Stephen Brown, S.J. (Dublin,
1919.)

over again during the last century, by Lever, Banim, Carleton, Griffin, George Moore, Shaw (see the contrasts of two types in *John Bull's Other Island*) , Liam O'Flaherty, Paul Vincent Carroll and others. Only two novelists have had inner access, Gerald O'Donovan, who was a lapsed priest, and Canon Sheehan; though in their novels one feels the defect inherent in a professional exclusiveness—the enclosed reference, the *a priori* assumptions: Sheehan can only draw priests, and only as priests, and poor minor characters—these are the best of all his characters, such as a chapel-woman (half-char, half-sacristan) or a beggar, or some bedridden old saint whom he must have often visited and dearly loved. O'Donovan's animus is a professional dissatisfaction with the Church: he had Modernist leanings.

An Arcane Profession

If from nothing else than the comparative failure of all these novelists to make us understand the source of the enormous political influence exercised by the priest—the moral influence presents no difficulty—one might, I suggest, be driven to look for it in the manner whereby he will always reduce to failure any analysis directed from only one angle of his nature. He is elusively twofold. His secret is that of all the arcane professions. It is impossible to isolate, in any one of his acts, his personal from his professional elements. What the military academy does to the cadet, what the law-schools do to the law student, the seminary does to the young cleric. Each one makes a sacrifice of his personal liberty, of the single-mindedness, or unity of his personality, in order to achieve the enlargement of power that comes with membership of a great professional caste. The cleric does this to an almost limitless extent. (Balzac recognises this in his *Curé de Campagne*, the better, I think, of the only two successful novels written about priesthood: the other, Fogazzaro's *Il Santo*. Some might add part of *Le Rouge et le Noir*.) Because of this sacrifice one can never see the priest exclusively as a priest: his human personality is dedicated but not suppressed; nor can we see him exclusively as a man: he has risen superior to normal human values, intercourse and sympathies, apart altogether from the fact that he is cut off from the lay-world by celibacy. In short, the priest, while apparently not *of* this world, is *in* it up to his neck.

If all this puts the priest in a doubtless sometimes troubling relationship to himself it puts him in a powerfully strategic relationship to the public. One can see this over and over in the puzzlement, sometimes the exasperation, of the layman at a loss to know where the human element and the professional element begins and ends. The priest, like the soldier, will always explain his public acts in professional terms, never in merely human terms; and although the angry layman—like Daniel O'Connell on more occasions than one—may privately sniff at clerical 'opportunism' he must hold his peace: because it may be so, and, in any case, the artillery of argument against him is colossal, not to mention the deadly power of the snipers and the discomfort of such fragmentation bombs as the cry of 'anti-clerical,' 'anti-God,' 'Red,' 'Leftist,' 'lay-bishop,' and that most devastating bomb of all, on which is chalked—'Yah! Intellectual!'*

* Here I use the words 'priest' and 'church' in a local sense; but the Church as a whole, or as we say 'the Vatican,' is the model for the Church in Ireland. See on this a very interesting essay: 'The Diplomacy of the Vatican,' by Daniel Binchy in *International Affairs*, January 1946, reprinted

Facing Both Ways

Let us state the fundamentals. The priest is fighting an immortal fight with mortal weapons. It is all very well for Lecky to say that the rise of Liberalism has declared the union of politics and theology an anachronism by pronouncing their divorce. The priest does not recognise divorce. For him the two worlds are inseparable; the kingdom of earth is but a battle-ground for the kingdom of heaven, and he will advance and retreat on that ground just like a soldier. No Irish priest, for example, objects to lay-control of education on principle—there is no such theological principle: when he thinks about the laity what he considers is the quality of its thought in the political temper of its times. Maynooth accepted a large measure of lay-control in 1795, through those constant inspections and visitations; and from a foreign Government at that. In 1799 the entire board of bishops at Maynooth agreed to subject *all* Catholic bishops to the *visa* of that foreign Government, which is surely the apex of lay-control? From its foundation it promised unswerving loyalty to that inspecting Government and installed professors guaranteed to maintain fanatically that this loyalty was

in *The Bell*, May 1946. 'The Vatican as a religious Power and the Vatican as a political Power cannot really be separated, but for a great many purposes they have to be distinguished. . . . The relation between politics and morality is an extremely difficult problem, and I do not believe that the Papacy, any more than any other Power, has succeeded in solving it. One result of this is that papal pronouncements on questions of international morality have to be made with an eye to the repercussions of such statements on the interest of the Church, not merely in the world as a whole but in one particular area; hence the tendency so often noted in such pronouncements, to enunciate only the most general principles. Again the necessity of considering the interests of the Catholic Church as a whole in a changing society leads to what may be called flexibility—or, if you prefer, opportunism—in various aspects of papal policy. More important still the wider view which is generally taken in the Curia often comes into conflict with local nationalism."

dogmatic. In short, the Catholic Church in Ireland, as such, does not—within the broadest limits of human justice, and indeed often tolerating human and clerical persecution to a degree astonishing to the layman—care a rap about the political Nation. It watches and waits and bargains all the time. It is a human institution in its political relationships; it may be guided by Heaven, but it must be wise in a human way. It does not engage personally in the human struggle, but wherever power emerges it will follow after—to bargain with it. It is, as a Church, superior to all merely human sympathies, however it may severally be agonised by the chaos of life and affairs about it. It will condemn the patriot to-day and do its heavenly business with him to-morrow—if he wins: but if the patriot counts on his support until he does win he is unreasonable if only because he would himself, probably, be the first to resent the interference of the Church on some other occasion. It is thus no exaggeration to say that the patriot, fighting for his country, hoping for success, must, if condemned by the Church, and if a loyal son of the Church, gamble his soul on a purely human victory. His dilemma contains an immortal irony. It rarely amuses those involved.

Obey—or Sin?

There can be no arguing about this. The law of obedience is binding. The layman must abide by the rules or, like Ivan Karamazov, 'hand back the ticket.' In 1922, for example, when a Civil War was raging in Ireland between the 'Republican' forces of Mr. de Valera and the 'National' forces of the Free State Government the Ordinary of the Diocese of Cork issued a Pastoral warning to his flock that: 'According to the declaration of the bishops of Ireland the killing of National soldiers is murder'; and that priests were doing their duty in refusing the sacraments to those who disobeyed. Any Catholic who disobeyed—and they numbered thousands—sinned. The Ordinary of a diocese may, so to speak, 'invent' a mortal sin by laying down a new rule at any moment. At this time the Ordinary of the Archdiocese of Dublin has declared it a mortal sin for Catholics deliberately to send their children, without his express permission, to Dublin University (non-Catholic). There are in this only four alternatives open to the devout: to obey without question as most do; to obey and appeal to Rome—a tedious and unpromising process which nobody has tried; to evade, e.g. by sending their children to Oxford or Cambridge, as a few do, or by transferring their residence outside the border of the Archdiocese to a diocese where the Ordinary has not made the same rule; or, lastly, he may rebel. The priest does not, however, often press the laity too hard. He prefers persuasions, he bides his time, he is infinitely patient. He allows the fullest interpretation to Burke's, 'It is no inconsiderable part of wisdom to know how much of an evil ought to be tolerated.'

Priests and Education

Let us pursue this illustration which has come our way. The University question is informative. It first appeared in the 1840's so that it is an old question now, though it was then, for Ireland, a rather late introduction to a problem that had long troubled other countries in Europe—the accommodation of Church and State in education. It falls into two stages. The operative date for the first stage is 1849. With the ending of the Penal Laws and the arrival

of Catholic Emancipation the British Government wished
to found a University in Ireland for the mass of the people. Peel proposed and founded in 1849 what came to be
known as Queen's Colleges. They were non-denomina-
tional, under secular control, and no provision was made
for teaching philosophy or history according to Catholic
viewpoints. The younger idealists and rebels (the Young
Irelanders) would have welcomed any scheme which
would provide higher education for the people; the bishops and O'Connell rejected it; and when the scheme developed in spite of them, the bishops laboured to keep
the middle-classes from sending their children to these
Queen's Colleges. We cannot here discuss this complex
and controversial question in detail. We can only consider
the one point before us. And, on that head, it is evident
that the refusal of the bishops to tolerate the Queen's Colleges was a perfectly legitimate and proper refusal. They
had been condemned on all sides, by Catholic laymen in
Ireland, by the Catholic bishops, by Conservative members of the House of Commons. All that this stage of the
question offers is a good illustration of the normal and
legitimate influence of the priest in the political arena.

Priest vs. Priest

The operative date for the second stage is 1852 when
Cardinal Paul Cullen persuaded John Henry Newman to
come to Dublin and found a Catholic University in opposition to Peel's 'godless colleges.' Newman had a very
sad time of it with the Irish bishops, and he soon found
himself at loggerheads even with Cardinal Cullen—over
the amount of control, if any, which the laity might be
permitted in the Catholic University. He saw that Cullen

was utterly suspicious of the rebelly spirit then alive in Irish political thought, what His Grace called 'Young Irelandism.' 'Dr. Cullen,' Newman wrote to a friend, 'seems to think that Young Irelandism is the natural product of the lay mind everywhere, if let to grow freely': and as a corollary would not tolerate almost *any* measure of lay-control. To this Newman could never agree: he said that if Dr. Cullen's views were to prevail the University would 'simply be priest-ridden. . . . I mean men who do not know literature and science will have the direction of the teaching. I cannot conceive the professors taking part in this. They will be simply scrubs.' And, again,—

'On both sides of the Channel the deep difficulty is the jealousy and fear which is entertained in high quarters of the laity. . . . Nothing great or living can be done except when men are self-governed and independent.'

The whole of Newman's relationship with the Irish clergy in that scheme for the establishment of a Catholic University in Ireland might be studied to great advantage by anybody interested in how the internal politics of the Catholic Church work out in practice. He found, without ever fully understanding it, that there does exist a permanent and positive clerical antipathy to the laity. This antipathy is very natural, as it seems to me, considering that the clergy are devoted to but one world—the next; and the interest of the laity is divided between this world and the next. Newman's weakness was that he was magnificently understanding and tolerant of the laity, especially for a man whose self-chosen epitaph was to be such a splendid gesture of contempt for this mortal coil: *Ex Umbris et Imaginibus in Veritatem* (From Shadows and Imaginings to the Truth). But Cardinal Cullen was not tolerant or sympa-

thetic. He was a prince; and he believed in ruling his subjects firmly. 'Poor Dr. Cullen,' Newman wrote of him, 'I
should not wonder if he is quite mastered by anxiety. The
great fault I find with him is that he makes no one his
friend, because he will confide in nobody and be consider-
ate to nobody. Everyone feels that he is emphatically close;
and while this conduct repels would-be friends it fills enemies with vague suspicions of possible conspiracies on his
part against Bishops, priests and the rights of Saint Patrick.
And he is as vehement against the Young Irelanders as
against the MacHaleites, and against the MacHaleites as
against the English.' That aloofness or suspicion flowed
towards Newman even to the point of rudeness, chiefly, I
think, because Newman would not hold the same attitude
towards the laity: though, in justice to Cullen it may
merely have been that he was bored by J. H. N. In the end,
as we know, tolerant Newman was got rid of by an opposition which whether coarse and vulgar (his own words), or
suave and subtle, was always relentless.

Priest vs. Laity

This antipathy to the laity certainly was, to some extent,
Anglade and Delahogue and MacHale and 'J. K. L.' all
over again: a political French-born terror of the 'Red
Spectre,' as the official biographer of Maynooth has called
it. It was not just Dr. Cullen's personal experiences in
Rome that lay behind this episcopal distrust of the layman and the rebel—he had seen the Republican Mazzini
take possession of Vatican property, and had personally
saved the College of Propaganda by persuading the American Minister to float the Stars and Stripes over it—Dr.
MacHale was just as adamant. 'There should no longer be

any doubt or ambiguity regarding the *exclusive* right of the bishops to legislate and to make all appointments.' (*Letters.* February 20th 1852.) In the century before, that devoted Catholic John Keogh, with Tone, had developed a scheme for a Catholic Seminary, and had been met, to Keogh's fury (and he was the mildest of men), by precisely the same absolute refusal to trust the laity. Keogh could not understand this. He thought it unreasonable. And humanly speaking it was unreasonable. But there the churchman slips away from us; for what has 'humanly speaking' to do with him? The bishops distrusted the Keogh-Tone collaboration, and from their point of view, considering Tone's French sympathies, very naturally so. In short it is obvious that although Dr. Cullen had a political antipathy to the Young Irelanders, as Dr. Egan had to the United Irishmen, nobody will ever pin down Dr. Cullen's distrust of his people to a purely secular political—not to speak of anti-nationalist—bias.

After all, when Newman returned to England he met precisely the same distrust of the laity in Cardinal Manning. Liberalism was in the air. Newman feared that Mill and Darwin and Huxley were undermining traditional belief. So might Manning, but he relied on the lymph of authority. Newman was an intellectual; his whole turn of mind was speculative and analytical; he foresaw that not authority but knowledge, not an absolutist church but a teaching church working hand in hand with an educated and independent-minded laity, was the only possible answer to the agnostic danger. It is a matter of record that when he raised such questions, to answer them, the priests, whether of England or Ireland, mopped and mowed and clutched their crucifixes as if he were introducing Beelzebub in person to a gullible and incompetent laity. (This

is the usual contempt of the professional for the layman.)
The laity welcomed Newman's fighting attitude. New
ideas were pouring in on them in the streets and the clubs
and the universities and men like W. G. Ward and the
future Lord Acton simply had to have access to the replies.
Newman had said, 'Great changes before now have taken
place in the Church's course and new aspects of her aborig-
inal doctrines have suddenly come forth,' and the layman
wanted to know what those new aspects were and what
light they threw on modern scientific and biblical re-
search. But the story of this long struggle between this
enquiring mind of a harassed laity and the traditionally
suspicious church has been told several times, including
the melancholy climax when Newman was denounced in
Rome and delated to the Holy See, as the agent of Catholic
Liberalism in England! If time has since proved Newman
right and Manning wrong, and if poor Newman meantime
suffered agonies of mind and soul, well, that is but the
story of the patriot all over again; and many and many a
patriot has had to be just as agile as Newman, in a different field, to evade destruction.

Priest vs. Patriot

In Ireland the struggle was not on an intellectual plane.
There, politics entered into it much more, because the
struggle circled around much more primitive and passionate questions—such as, 'When is it lawful for a suppressed nation to rebel?', a question to which, of course,
there is no real answer. Fenianism was rife in Ireland in
the 1860's—the latest successors to the Young Irelanders
and the United Irishmen. An entry in O'Neill Daunt's
Diary puts their dilemma succinctly:

'September 12th, 1865: When the priests condemned Fenianism in the confessional and refused the sacraments to persons connected with it many of the Fenian youths of Cork gave up going to confession to priests who had been educated at Maynooth; but some of them confessed to priests brought up in foreign seminaries.'

That date has a special and interesting significance. In the chapter called 'The Rebel' I pointed out that the spirit of rigorism, often called Jansenism, imported from France into Maynooth could not have outlasted the 1850's there. This is true; but another fresh element had meanwhile entered Ireland, this time from Italy, which gave this rigorism in morals a new lease of life in politics. This element was the loyalist, ultramontanist response to Garibaldi and the threat to the Papal Dominions, which, as we know, were ultimately reduced to the extent of the Vatican City. On this period Wilfrid Ward says in his biography of Cardinal Wiseman:

'The tendency of a section of the French clergy, ever since 1793, to conceive of a war between the Church and the age, the age being identified with "Liberalism" and the "Revolution," reappeared in a more marked form than heretofore. The circumstances of the hour made the same tendency strong in Rome itself; and the animosity which many of us remember, against the very word "Liberalism" reached its acutest stage. It was from 1860 to 1870 that the term "liberal Catholic" came to be used in so invidious a sense . . . The controversy . . . between the Catholics who were anxious to meet half-way, and thereby to influence the spirit of the times, and those who held that the Zeitgeist of the 19th century is essentially a spirit of revolt against the Christian faith was (for practical purposes) decided, for the moment, in favour of the latter.'

The Syllabus and Encyclicals of 1864, associating the Roman question with godless principles, helps us to understand the force of O'Neill Daunt's entry of 1865. It is interesting that it is the Maynooth-trained priests who condemned the Fenians, whereas the foreign-trained priests forgave them. But in all probability Maynooth did not have any intelligent idea of what was going on and was affected chiefly by a warm-hearted sense of loyalty to the Holy Father. The connection between the Fenians and the Garibaldians was slight; and nobody knew about it anyway but a few conspirators in Ireland, America and Italy. He would therefore be a very shallow observer who would say that this condemnation was either purely political, or purely theological.

One cannot, I repeat, isolate the elements. The priest is indissolubly of heaven and earth: which is what makes him so slow to commit himself in any earthly fight, and—I say it quite objectively and without a trace of irony, for he is, from his point of view, quite right—it is this also that makes him come out from his cautious seclusion only when he finds the flood in full spate around him. The priest was slow to support O'Connell. He was slow to support the Home Rule movement. (Another entry of O'Neill Daunt's *Diary*, September 1870, speaks of a letter from T. D. Sullivan complaining about 'the small number of priests who have heretofore joined the Home Rule Movement.') He was slow to support the Sinn Fein movement. And so, likewise, he is, generally, slow also to condemn. It is the layman in politics who forces the priest into politics, or, if one prefers, urges him before him—always *at his peril*. Conversely is it not the layman who complains when the priest enters politics without him?

A small, but telling, illustration of the Church's indifference to 'the Nation' as such is offered by the Irish Language Revival. Enthusiasts sometimes complain that the Church in Ireland is not behind the Revival Movement. Once again, why should it be? And if, historically, the priest has been rather opposed to the Language Movement than otherwise, why should he not be? All one's sympathies, mine do at any rate, will go out to that courageous man Dr. O'Hickey, Professor of Gaelic at Maynooth, who was sacked by Maynooth in 1909 because he fought openly for the introduction of compulsory Irish into the National University, who tried to fight his case to Rome, and who, like many another, died without receiving any decision. But if the Catholic Church in Ireland then regarded, as it apparently did (and still regards), the Language Revival as unlikely to be of assistance to it, it is fully entitled to withhold its official support. The Language enthusiast, like every other enthusiast, may rest assured that the Church in Ireland will, like Lord Chesterfield to Dr. Johnson, throw him a rope only when he is on dry land. And if the somewhat dampened enthusiast could imagine himself transmogrified into a board of bishops he will agree that he, in their place, would do just the same, or else his imagination has not worked hard enough.

Priest vs. Statesman

The modern Irish politician has, I think, only recently begun to understand all this. And I should not be surprised if the Church in Ireland itself is only beginning to see the position clearly. There have been some burnings of fingers on both sides, and there is an old inheritance of distrust. In 1946, when the primary teachers went on strike, the Archbishop of Dublin made it evident that his sympathies were with them: the Government absolutely refused to accept His Grace as intermediary. When Bishop Dignan produced his scheme for a comprehensive system of Social Insurance in 1945 the Minister for Local Government repulsed it acidly. A weighty Report from a Commission on Vocational Representation, which had been sitting for years under the chairmanship of the Bishop of Galway, was the occasion of some sharp exchanges with another Minister; and the Report has since been silently interred. What do these three incidents mean? Do they mean that the priest, now that we have our own government, is only too willing to take a hand in purely secular political and social questions? Hardly. Education has always been a rope pulled from two ends. Vocational Representation would involve large political changes that might affect the influence of the Church. That leaves us with just one example not directly of clerical interest, Social Insurance. In that case the priest was refreshingly more advanced and humane than the politician who rebuffed him. Do these rebuffs suggest, on the other hand, that the State is becoming jealous of its autonomy? There is so far enough evidence to suspect, only, that while the politician shows no sign of wanting to move ahead of his guide (and in Social Insurance he lags well behind), one could not call them happy fellow-travellers.

The extent to which there is an alliance between Church and State in modern Ireland is debatable. I think the word 'alliance' is too strong: better, some such word as 'junction'—to indicate the opposite of the liberal vocabulary about a 'disjunction' of those two central powers. But either a tacit alliance or a casual junction would be equally deplorable, and no wise Catholic—least of all the Church itself—could desire it. In Ireland the Church holds her power by the old mediaeval bond of Faith. She does not need political techniques, as the Church in other more secularised countries does; and if she does not need them, she must be held unjustified in using them. The Catholic Church in Ireland therefore is, or should be, *immune*, to borrow a word from Lord Acton—'The Pope is at the head of a great *immunitas*, like many other prelates.' Immune she should remain. It was Acton, again, who insisted that in all secular States the existence of great classes, nobles, clergy, etc., limits the State power; and he deplored the fact that at the date in which he was writing (January 1862) the 'great class of clergy is the mere instrument of the sovereign. Liberty,' he concluded, 'consists *in radice* in the preservation of an inner sphere exempt from State power.' A Church, overtly or tacitly, deliberately or unwittingly, in alliance or in junction with the State, must sooner or later become identified in the public mind with the State, and must cease to be an 'inner sphere': it must cease to be exempt from criticism of that with which—or through which—it works. It need not be added that the quality of the liberty which will exist inside any 'inner sphere' will, of course, depend on how civilised and humanised that envelope, that sanctuary itself is. This is the great test of the Catholic Church in Ireland to-day.

Priest vs. Writer

In Ireland, to-day, priests and laity rest at ease—with one qualification. Only one group is held at arm's length, the writers or intellectuals. They, at a far, far remove from that unapproachably great man whose name we have invoked several times, Newman, see that the intellectual

struggle is upon Ireland's doorstep. They want questions
to be raised, and answered. The Church relies on the
weapon of rigid authority. It could do that as long as it
was concerned with an Ireland protected and sheltered
from the world. The writers see clearly that this isolation
is now a dream. Walls of censorship have been erected to
keep out books and films that raise awkward questions.
Practically every Irish writer of note has at one time or
another been thrown to the lambs, i.e. in the interests of
the most unsophisticated banned in his own country, some
over and over again.* But the air is uncensorable. Vulgarity
and cheapness are not censored. Films are censored only
for blatantly objectionable things: their triviality, their
debasing cheapness of thought, their tinsel dreams infect
the most remote villages. Above all a constant flow and
reflow of emigrants flood in the world outside with all its
questions, challenges and bright temptations. In so far as
the priest seems content he seems to the Irish writer to be
either excessively cautious or excessively lazy, or to be
making exactly the same mistake that Cardinal Manning
made in England in the 60's. One may, for instance, be
appalled to think that there is not in Ireland to-day a single layman's Catholic periodical to which one could apply
the adjective 'enquiring,' or even 'intelligent,' in the sense
in which it could have been applied to Newman's *Ram-
bler;* and that with the exception of one professional or-
gan and one admirable Jesuit quarterly, the clerical pa-
pers are all trivial—a state of affairs that might almost

---

* Among typical writers who have at one time or another been banned
(not all the books of each) are Shaw, George Moore, Sean O'Casey, Liam
O'Flaherty, Frank O'Connor, Kate O'Brien, Francis Stuart, Elizabeth Connor, Austin Clarke, Norah Hoult, Louis Lynch D'Alton, Con O'Leary, Sean
O'Faolain, *etc.* Some have since been 'unbanned.' Thousands of non-Irish
writers have been banned including some of the most interesting Catholic
writers: e.g. Graham Greene.

justify the Irish intellectual in echoing Newman's famous phrase about the 'temporary suspense of the *Ecclesia Docens.*' There is no *Blackfriars,* no *Dublin Review,* no *Commonweal,* no periodical remotely like Emmanuel Mounier's *Esprit.* The tragedy of all this is, of course, that the priest and the writer ought to be fighting side by side, if for nothing else than the rebuttal of the vulgarity that is pouring daily into the vacuum left in the popular mind by the dying out of the old traditional life. But there can be no such common ground as long as the priest follows the easy way of authority instead of discussion, takes the easy way out by applying to all intellectual ideas the test of their effect on the poor and the ignorant. Above all, how can there be common ground when even the least observant can see on all sides that the primary attitude of the layman to the priest is less one of co-operation than of a businesslike caution. It does not pay in business to adopt a too-independent attitude to the Church.

An 'Established' Church?

There are times, I confess, when I am tempted to go much further than this; when I feel inclined to believe that the Church in Ireland is betraying the ideal of religion as the politicians so often seem to betray the ideal of the nation. Religion, as Newman saw long ago, even so early as in his Anglican days, finds its true power in the pervasive influence of the sacraments, in its apostolical ministry, and in the fellowship of the faithful with it. It is no part of the function of a church to make policemen do its work, and that is precisely what the Church does in Ireland when it works through the State, by means of political lobbying, to tighten up the Licensing Laws, or to

enforce a Censorship of books, or to control public amusements such as dancing, or to censor the Cinema, or to prevent Birth Control, or to abolish Divorce. This is either
the spiritual arm abdicating in favour of the temporal; or
the spiritual arm pushing the temporal arm before it. It
savours, in fact, of a disguised Establishment of inordinate
power. It need hardly be said that there are plenty of
Irishmen only too willing to be pushed into the field as
standard-bearers; some because of genuine religious fer-
vour, some because it pays; and it is chiefly these laymen
who do the public work. We have Catholic Women's Fed-
erations, Catholic Boy Scouts, Catholic Seamen, Catholic
Girl Guides, Catholic Commercial Clubs, Catholic Actors,
Catholic Rescue Workers, Catholic Social Services, Catholic Writers, Catholic Libraries, and so on—all in a country so predominantly Catholic that the word seems to
suffer a rather unnecessary repetition. There is hardly a
field in which this system of an organised laity does not
function so efficiently that other Catholics might well begin to wonder if priests in Ireland have any necessary function at all left other than to administer the sacraments
once a week. It is natural that, in these circumstances, the
ecclesia docens should not see any need to work hard: and
natural that the more intelligent Catholic should feel that
he will look to it in vain for intellectual guidance. I will
give a small illustration of the extent and folly of the
system and this pressure. The present writer, a Catholic,
once belonged to a little group of Catholic laymen who
met regularly to discuss modern problems. The first rule
of this Society—it was formulated in self-defense by the
more timid—was that under no circumstances must any
word be spoken outside the Society about what was said
inside it.

From all this the reader will draw whatever conclusion he thinks suitable: that Catholicism in Ireland is as solid as a rock, and knows it, or that it is not quite as solid as a rock and knows it; that the Church in Ireland has done its work well, or that it has done it a little too well, or that it is not doing it well at all; that it is easy to be a Catholic in Ireland, or extremely difficult; that the Church is wide-awake, as it evidently is satisfied that it is, or that it is in the condition of the Sleeping Beauty. But one thing is undeniable. To intellectual Catholicism Ireland contributes virtually nothing; which, it would appear, is but another case of the balance of the weak Challenge and the weak Response. It is also another illustration of the effect of being at the end of the queue; for by being there we both lose and gain, enjoy and escape—have no nightingales, but also have no serpents; no moles, also no ballet; no Communist intelligentsia, but also no Catholic intelligentsia. Is it our happy dream that we have no need of either?

There is one minor point on which the modern observer, especially the foreign visitor to Eire, should be forewarned. He will see ten times as many priests in Eire as he will in England or Wales: he may therefore think the country over-lavishly supplied with priests. There are actually just about as many priests in England and Wales as there are in Ireland. (I follow the figures given in *Whitaker's Almanack*.) Furthermore, in relation to the Catholic population of England and Wales, and the Catholic population of Eire, there are nearly twice as many priests per head in England and Wales. That is, there is, roughly, one priest per 770 Catholics in Eire, and one priest per 470 Catholics in England and Wales. (In Scotland each priest has to serve about 870 Catholics.) If we take the popula-

tion absolutely, without regard to religion, there is in England and Wales only one priest per 8,700 people. Therefore, if in England and Wales one does not meet many
Catholic priests, and in Eire one meets far more, that is
because, in Eire, almost the entire lay population is Catholic. It is natural that in a country composed mainly of
Catholics (or of Hindus, or of Mormons) one will meet
many clergy of those persuasions. One will not say of such
countries that they are 'over-crowded' with priests, though
one may, to be sure, if one so desires, say that these places
are over-crowded with Catholics (or Hindus or Mormons).

The Writers

THREE creative events—the only kind of events that we are concerned with here—occurred in nineteenth-century Ireland. They were Catholic Emancipation, Land Reform, the Literary Revival. The first gave the vote to the masses and began modern parliamentary politics. From that came a series of Land Acts, which, bit by bit, changed a dependent tenantry into an independent yeomanry: this process is now almost completed. In the Literary Revival we get the summary of the whole of this transformation of an ancient race, first defeated, then depressed, then virtually stripped of its traditions, into a modern people—or a more or less modern people, for that process also continues, and is far from complete. The new literature did more than summarise, it was itself an active agent. It was more, far more, than a number of isolated writers 'expressing themselves.' It was a whole people giving tongue, and by that self-articulation approaching nearer than ever before to 'intellectual and imaginative freedom.'

Irish literature in Gaelic, like the Irish aristocracy, had received in the seventeenth century blows from which it never recovered. Being the literature of a caste it must die with the caste. What of it persisted into the eighteenth century, and in a ragtag-and-bobtail way into the nineteenth century, was the kind of survival which, less by its content than by its persistence, achieves honour mingled with pity—neither a healthy nor an honourable reception.

A literature, one feels, must justify itself on its literary merits, not a factitious appeal. An exclusively patriotic or nostalgic interest in literature is disgusting. It makes it of merely sentimental interest. It relegates it to the bottom drawer with baby's shoes and mother's wedding-veil. 'Look,' one says, with tears welling, 'this was written by one of our poor, down-trodden people in dark and evil days. We must always preserve it.' By all means, let us preserve everything, even the humblest and crudest implement of man; do not let us then give it a greater value than its historical value. Some of the Gaelic poetry written in the eighteenth century, by the last surviving members of the caste, has genuine merit; most of it has no merit; what has a real merit, and has proved it by its living, developing persistence—which is not a museum persistence—is the lore of the common people. That is vital. It has now gone underground; it is, so to speak, being forgotten *consciously;* it still beats like a great earth-throb in the subconsciousness of the race. The Irish language is thus become the runic language of modern Ireland. Only a dwindling few think overtly in it; all of us can, through it, touch, however dimly, a buried part of ourselves of which we are normally unaware; through Gaelic we remember ancestrally, are again made very old and very young. As compared with the literary survivals of the last two hundred years, the popular, vocal lore is in this way infinitely richer, more imaginative and more inspiring.

Modern Beginnings

The inspiration of the men who first set the modern literary revival on its way was nostalgic and sentimental. These men were the rebelly group known as the Young

Irelanders, whose rise we may date at the year 1845, by the first issue of their paper *The Nation*. They thus came after Catholic Emancipation, were contemporaneous with O'Connell, took part in the Tithe War, the fight for the Repeal of the Union of Britain and Ireland, the arguments over Education, the start of the land troubles, and welled over, through their successors, into the parliamentary fight in Westminster. They found a depressed and uneducated peasantry, saw the first great waves of emigration to America, and watched the dying-out of the native language. To them O'Connell, who, as a pragmatic politician, had no time for Gaelic and said that he saw it die without regret, was too materialist, too vulgar, too cheap, not idealist enough to build up the soul of the people.

'To them, in their own high idealism, his appeals on the score of Ireland's material poverty were almost base; they thought of glory, not of finance, and they ransacked the past that O'Connell had kicked aside. They tried to learn from little books the language O'Connell spoke as a child, and thereafter only when addressing the peasants of the western seaboards. They would meet on the roads old men who were to O'Connell so many votes and little else, and because of the memories these old men preserved they saw, behind the apparent illiteracy, the superficial roughness or even boorishness, something like the last rays of their sun-god. How angry they would have been to hear O'Connell called King of the Beggars—not because they could deny his kingship but because they felt themselves as the descendants of kings. These—Mangan, Davis, Gavan Duffy, Meagher, Mitchel, Doheny, and others—created in verse and prose, for they were all able men of letters, image after image of the legendary greatness of their people, and they appealed to the country in the name of its former glory.' *

* From *King of the Beggars*. O'Faolain. (Viking Press, 1938.)

All that I have already said about the way in which the
Rebel spends and wastes himself is true a hundredfold of
these men. They did not devote their great talents to literature: they devoted them to literature in the interests of
politics. Their interest was in functional literature, or as
we now call it *littérature engagée*. Their literary work
suffered accordingly; their political influence prospered.

Before a literary movement could develop in a strictly
literary way Irish writers had to purify literature of this
political impurity. The first historian of that later period
went so far, and rightly, as to define the process as one of
Dedavisisation—Thomas Davis being the outstanding cre-
ator of this politico-literary journalism of the 1840's. Yet,
in one way the Young Irelanders were wise in their generation: they insisted on the use of native material. To
show the absolute rightness of this let us look, very shortly,
at the good (and bad) example of one of their predecessors, the Cork poet Jeremiah Joseph Callanan, who died
in 1829.

A Transitional Poet

This poet is remembered to-day for ballads and songs
that propose him as the first really popular Irish poet writing in English: see his fine poem on 'Gougane Barra,' his
ballad 'The Revenge of Donal Cawm,' his translation of
some of the really good Gaelic songs of the eighteenth century, such as 'O say my brown Drimin, thou silk of the
kine,' or 'The Convict of Clonmel.' The truth is that in so
far as he is a popular poet he is popular in spite of himself,
almost by accident, and his history is a revelation of how
easily a poet may miss his true inspiration. At Trinity College he won his first recognition for a poem on, of all

things, 'Alexander's Restoration of the Spoils of Athens.'
He wrote a sycophantic poem in praise of George IV. For
years his models were English models. Byron was the 'bard
of my boyhood's love,' his 'eagle of song,' his 'fountain of
beauty.' In theory there was nothing wrong with all this.
In practice the effect on a young provincial Irishman was
not good: as one may see at one glance.

> The night was still, the air was balm,
> Soft dews around were weeping . . .

All that came of it, that is, were pleasant, pseudo-Byronic
verses of which one may say that none of them go very far
except in the sense that they all go much too far—from
home, from life, from reality:

> Thy name to this bosom
> Now sounds like a knell;
> My fond one, my dear one,
> For ever farewell.

A Byron could write light songs in that theme and make
them ring with passionate tenderness; not an unsophisticated Irish country lad pretending to be a Byron. Thus,
Callanan's most ambitious poem, and the poem in which
he took most pride, was 'The Recluse of Inchidony.' The
difference between something that is just a pose, and
something that is experienced may be seen in the comparison of eight lines of 'Inchidony' with eight lines of
'Childe Harold.' Here is Callanan:

> 'Tis a delightful calm. There is no sound
> Save the low murmur of the distant rill.
> A voice from heaven is breathing all around
> Bidding the earth and restless man be still.

> Soft sleeps the moon on Inchidony's hill
> And on the shore the shining ripples break
> Gently and whisperingly at Nature's will,
> Like some fair child that on its mother's cheek
> Sinks fondly to repose in kisses pure and meek.

Passing over the tired clichés, is there one speck of actual observation in all that? But see Byron, eye fixed on the object or on the memory:

> It is the hush of the night and all between
> Thy margin and the mountains dusk yet clear,
> Mellowed and mingling, yet distinctly seen
> Save darkened Jura, whose capped heights appear
> Precipitously steep. And drawing near
> There breathes a living fragrance from the shore
> Of flowers yet fresh with childhood. On the ear
> Drops the light drip of the suspended oar
> Or chirps the grasshopper one good-night carol more.

'The light drip of the suspended oar' is alone enough to mark the distinction. Callanan has not learned to revere the simple detail of life about him, that stuff of which all later Irish writers were to make their best work. He therein reflects the lack of pride of his century. He is, in fact, the counterpart in English of the irrealism of a great deal of eighteenth-century Gaelic verse, equally eager to escape reality.

The Romantic movement—of which, to make another essential point, all Irish rebellion (Tone and the Young Irelanders and the rest) is a reflection, and all Irish literature the offspring—let Callanan out of his dilemma. Scott had resurrected the clansman. It was part of the tradition to unearth old ballads. Bishop Percy's *Reliques of Ancient Poetry* had appeared in 1765. Joseph Ritson had been collecting old English songs since 1783. Joseph Walker's *Historical Memoirs of the Irish Bards* came in 1786. Charlotte Brooke brought out her *Ancient Irish Poetry* in 1789. Edward Bunting in Ireland had been collecting Irish folk-music since 1792. What to these was antiquity to Callanan was everyday life. Callanan looked about him and began finely to translate songs he had often listened to but, until now, never heard. He writes patronisingly of them, not recognising the gifts even as he took them, calling them 'the popular songs of the lower orders,' and saying, 'I present them to the public more as literary curiosities than on any other account.'

The Entrance of Realism

The point is made. The Irish writer was a provincial while he imitated slavishly and tried to write beyond his talents; he ceased to be a provincial when he wrote of what he knew and could describe better than anybody else. The Young Irelanders, then, were wise to attempt the same thing and by attempting it they set Irish literature on its true road. Their weakness and bad example was to subserve literature to opinions, to political dogmatising, to nationalist 'right' and 'wrong' which, by directing the eye away from the literary object to the political goal, introduced a new falsity and undid a certain amount of their appeal to realism. Their best writer was James Clarence Mangan, who profited to the full by their literary inspiration but who can only remotely be connected with their political propaganda.

The development of modern Irish literature since the 1840's might thus be described as a prolonged voyage of discovery, conducted by Irish writers, into the romantic

reality of Irish life, present and past. As their intimacy
with their material grows their absorption grows with it.
Sometimes they were delighted by what they found, sometimes repelled, always they were excited, for the nationalist spirit was at hand to excite the mind, even if it were
only to excite it to furious disagreements. This is the essential. Without the national thing—at any rate up to our
own day—an Irish writer was always in danger of becoming a provincial by becoming an imitator. He would not
merely take models, that is to say Russian, or French, or
German writers, and learn his trade from them, and be
excited constantly by the work of other men as every writer
is, and apply himself then to his own sort of life which he
knew so well: he would if he remained an imitator try to
be a man of another country and describe the life of another country, in which he must—outside of very special
circumstances—inevitably fail. The national thing gave
Irish writers the necessary resolution, or if they rejected
the political tenets of nationalism, the necessary excitement to find in Ireland the stuff of their work. George
Moore illustrates the double process. His special circumstances, his wealth mainly, made it possible for him to
transfer himself bodily, and to a great extent mentally,
out of Ireland as a very young man. What he learned in
France went into his naturalistic novels. The nationalist
excitement drew him back to Ireland, out of which he
got two excellent books, *Hail and Farewell* and *The Lake.*
The original Abbey Theatre would have been inconceiv-
able without the nationalist movement. And who, fifty
years before, would have met a young Irishman in a Paris
café and told him to go to the Aran Islands, as Yeats told
Synge, unless it had been for the purposes of some crack-
brained political conspiracy—which, it may be agreed,

would merely be 'the national thing' under another form.

That meeting of two Irishmen in Paris, agreeing that the life of these most remote and barren Aran Islands was full material for literature, is a parable that marks the final stage in the growth of the Irish mind. Plenty of people before Synge had written about Irish life—Lever, Lover, the Banims, Gerald Griffin, hosts of hardly-known poets and novelists. Only the exceptions, and the exception does not include any I have mentioned bar Lever, are readable to-day. The explanation becomes obvious immediately one opens their books. They never really got down to it. They are sometimes regionalists, exploiting the 'local colour' of the wild Irish scene; sometimes they are patriots, using Irish life as a peg for opinions; they are, at other times, mere literary dilettantes, exploiting Ireland as 'a subject.' Examples are the novelists Gerald Griffin and Charles Kickham, and the fashionable versifier Dick Millikin. Each novelist is a kind of diluted Walter Scott, never really sure of the absolute interest of his material and, to make up for this imaginary lack, padding it up with some kind of contemporary (and so passing) social or political interest or literary fashion. (I say nothing of 'the stage-Irishman,' which is a form of exploitation too obvious to need comment.) It was an entirely new thing for men to realise the full and complete dignity of the simplest life of the simplest people. Once they had acknowledged that then they were free to do anything they liked with it in literature—treat it naturalistically, fantastically, romantically, see it in any light they chose. They had conquered their material by accepting it.

In the most creative period of Anglo-Irish literature (from about 1890 to about 1920) the writers saw Irish life, in the main, romantically. It was as a poetic people that they introduced themselves to the world, and it is as a poetic people that we are still mainly known abroad. The peasant-plays of the Abbey Theatre, even when supposedly realistic, held still the charm of external novelty —dress, speech, situation, humour—and were bathed in that sense of natural wonder which is best illustrated by the plays of Synge. Towards the end of the period a satirical note made itself felt, and in the plays of Sean O'Casey—all the natural wonder being removed, for they are set in the Dublin slums—we were left with an unassuaged realism. The Novel, budding from the work of George Moore and James Joyce, and profoundly affected by the French and Russian realists, likewise began to hold a far from indulgent mirror up to nature. When the revolutionary period of 1916-1922 ended miserably in a civil war, romance died completely. Most Irish literature since 1922 has been of an uncompromising scepticism, one might even say ferocity. I will quote but one example, the novels of Liam O'Flaherty.

Emancipation . . .

Once the people began to see themselves in these various lights it could only be a matter of time before they became intellectually and imaginatively free—free of their own feeble or flattering self-opinions, free of all sorts of assumptions about themselves, native or foreign; free of easy assumptions about others. But this experience could hardly be painless, and this process, too, is far from finished. It is a matter of record that the Irish theatre has probably seen more riots than any other, and it is probable that a greater proportion of native writers of note has been banned in Ireland than in Russia.

What has, for the moment, happened is that which I mentioned at the close of the chapter on 'The New Peasantry' and to which I can now advert more fully. The Irish people have entered into the last stage of that process of urbanisation which began when the Norman invasion sowed towns and town-life all over a mainly pastoral country. From the very beginning of our history this is a process which we have resisted. Even now we resist it still. We are rooted in the land and in individualism. We have always feared towns and organised society. We have felt them as spear-heads of life-ways which are complex, troublesome and challenging. To-day we call those life-ways 'foreign' and in trying to impose a peasant life-way on the towns we try to exclude anything which the peasant (especially the Catholic peasant) does not understand. Literature is, naturally, one of those things which the peasant looks upon with the greatest suspicion. That the poor fellow's defences are meanwhile being utterly undermined by the vulgarities of the cinema, the radio, trashy books, cheap amusements, 'foreign' fashions of every sort and the chase for easy money, and by the effects of a hand-over-fist emigration to industrial Britain under the worst social conditions, he does not realise in the least. He thinks himself safe behind formal religion, formal censorships, and an emotional Nationalism that is, at least, a quarter of a century out of date.

. . . and Resistance

A simple illustration is his attitude to the Anglo-Irish tradition. He thinks he has conquered it whereas in fact it has absorbed him. He speaks of it sometimes as 'alien,' as, of course,—the name says so—it is as much as the Norman

tradition was. He sometimes goes even farther with this
'alien' tradition: he is tempted to disown it altogether.
But how can he? He is proud, for example, of the city of
Dublin, however much it may, on occasion, irk him to remember that it was built, stone for stone, by 'aliens'—
Danes, Normans, Tudors or Cromwellians, mingled with
the old native blood. He knows that Ireland has won honour all over the world through such names as Bishop
Berkeley, Jonathan Swift, Oliver Goldsmith, Edmund
Burke, Oscar Wilde, Bernard Shaw, William Butler
Yeats. Without them and so many other Anglo-Irish
writers—for though a name be Celtic, like O'Flaherty
or O'Connor or O'Casey, the tradition is always one—he
would be very naked indeed. Nor can he develop a blood-
test for Pure Eireanns, not with such un-Celtic national
heroes as Tone, Parnell and De Valera. Unable to make
up his mind to accept the warp and woof of history, he
keeps on nagging at the Anglo-Irish—rather like the silly
wife of a great public man, proud of her husband's repu-
tation and yet jealously wishing that he could have made it
while staying mousily at home listening to her talking
about the neighbours and her gall-stones. And all this is
so because he wants to take over the town-life the Anglo-
Irish bequeathed to him and does not know how to handle
it.

This conflict is persistent in modern Ireland. It is most
clearly typified in the class which we call the New Middle
Classes or the New Bourgeoisie. Mathematically-speaking
this term 'Middle Classes' is impossible, because we have
no Upper Classes—apart from the remnants of the old
Anglo-Irish aristocracy who, unfortunately, are too few,
too disgusted, too dispirited, or too indifferent to take
part, as a body, in political life. We call the peasants-in-

the-towns the Middle Classes only because they have taken over the deplorable mentality and outlook of that type as we know it in Britain and the Continent. This, however painful, is understandable—for all the good understanding does to the country which has to endure a new, rude and crude citizenry in from the heather: simple folk who have shot up like Jack on the Beanstalk from the humblest circumstances; mostly by the same lucky chances that favour men of enterprise, ability or mere cunning at the turn of the tide of any revolution. They have mostly profited by the Irish Government's eagerness to develop native industries, frequently even getting virtual monopolies of the home market behind a tariff-wall. Nobody begrudged them their luck or their sudden-found wealth; and many of them have worked hard to exploit their fortunate chances, though not all, for not all have given good value to the public and many are mere middle-men who contribute nothing to the country but a distributing service at a high cost. What *is* hard to endure is the combination, in this class, of vulgarity and insincerity. Even the vulgarity one could forgive. How could we expect a stock so long suppressed to blossom suddenly into a class of cultured men? The insincerity of the brute is unforgiveable. For in the feverish pursuit of wealth this class seems to have thrown aside all their old, fine rural traditions and every standard but Success. They indulge shamelessly in lobbying, political wire-pulling, do not stop at open corruption, kow-tow to clerical influence, make a constant parade of patriotism and piety, never utter, rarely support, and (with some honourable exceptions) do nothing to create an independent public opinion. Their influence on political and social life is pervasive; they have no organised opposition except Labour, which, in a country

predominantly agricultural, is not strong, and is itself in
any case not yet trained to think. I do not wish to paint
a villainous picture. On the contrary these individuals are
the most pleasant and sociable rascals in the world. They
are kind and charitable, and what is known as 'good
sports,' so that no stranger or native who does not use his
political uncommon-sense would think them other than
a splendid addition to the community, instead of, as they
are, a splendid subtraction from the community—in the
shape of fat profits at public expense. The most engag-
ing, and infuriating thing about these individuals is that
they are tremendously patriotic. What they are doing for
Ireland is their constant theme-song; no mention being,
of course, made of the percentage charged. After all, are
they not the sons of the men who fought for 'seven hundred years' for Liberty? The fact is as undeniable as the
profits.

If, however, from these harsh remarks the reader might
conclude that the arrival of the peasant in the towns is to
be deplored he would conclude wrongly. They are part
of the inevitability of history; and to deplore the inevitable would be a folly. The only sensible attitude any
intelligent Irishman can adopt towards them is that of a
parent with a family come to that tiresome age when they
can no longer be treated quite like children and cannot
yet be treated as adults. One alternatively thinks fondly
of them as they were when they were dependent and
biddable, wishes to heaven they would grow up quickly,
and wonders why the devil one ever had them. One is
by turns patient with them and furious with them, sym-
pathises with them and loathes the sight of them. (Parents
do not always admit this but parents do not always tell
the truth.) There they are; and we must put up with

them; and they will never know when they do grow up what beasts they were in their teens; just as nobody will ever realise what a tedious and sordid period it was in Ireland between about 1925 and whenever, in whatever century, an indigenous, tolerable and cultivated urban life will have at last developed out of the nursery of time.

The 'Feel' of Ireland

And now I may at last attempt to say something which I have been tempted to say several times earlier in this record. Over and above all that one may observe visually in the Irish achievement there is that intangible thing which every traveller in every country finds it the most difficult thing to describe and which is nevertheless the most important thing of all. I can only refer to it, inadequately, as the 'feeling' of a country. The feel of Italy, the feel of France, the feel of Ireland, the feel of England, is the very sap of the life of these countries. You get it immediately you land in these countries. You get it from the cabby, the porter, the policeman, the man of whom you ask the way, the look of a café or a pub, the colouring of the houses, the monuments, the noises, the tempo, the way a man carries his clothes, the way a girl dresses, the way the people laugh, or do not. You get it where the conjurer seems to get pigeons, out of the air. Ireland has a distinct feel. Because of it we can only say, 'with all her faults we love her still.' (Which does not prevent us from hating her with a bitter hatred just as often). Here is a country with few monuments and these most dearly paid for: few traditions that have projected themselves; no palaces here, no triumphal arches, hardly a statue outside Dublin, no provincial Pinacoteca, or Piazza Dante or ancient amphitheatre, or towering cathedral, no Siena or Rouen or Bath, no gay café life, no mellow Dorset towns, few, if any really pretty villages, no clever cooking, no wines . . . the list of things that we have not that other lands have, or have had, is long. And, yet, that good 'feel' is there. It is as if Italy had never had all which the eye can see that has made her famous; and yet still had all her traditions (unprojected in those forms and shapes and institutions), her homogeneity, her charm, her people—pleasant, friendly, kindly, courteous, warm, passionate, cynical, lazy, loveable, lying and easygoing. And, indeed, to-day there is only a thin kind of bridge, like a rope-bridge, between all that past greatness of Italy and her present existence, and still the race remains and endows its country with an enviable atmosphere. Ireland has achieved likewise a certain character that draws her children home and that pleases visitors and, though in itself indescribable, it defines her. Naturally the visitor sees it both most keenly and most sketchily. One has to live in a country to know why it can simultaneously be true that, for example, Italy's feel and character could be powerful and affecting and yet so devoted a lover of Italy as Carducci could say *La nostra patria è vile!*

It is an extraordinary victory for Irishmen that despite so terrible and so depressing a history, they have yet succeeded in emerging as, to mention only one characteristic, an attractively good-humoured people. A great deal of nonsense has been written about Irish charm. That too exists. It may exist maddeningly—for behind it is much that is not charm—but it exists. There is a good deal of intolerance (born of insufficient inexperience and a narrow concept of religion) behind our kindness; but the kindness is the pervasive thing. And so on. When this feeling for life or feeling of life in time projects itself in more *things*—institutions, objects, conventions—we shall all be happier and be able to lead richer and more varied lives. At present for the *homme moyen sensuel* Ireland is a Paradise of sport and good companionship; but for him alone, outside of Dublin, that immense Anglo-Irish gift. If, by now, the reader has not begun to see why this might naturally be the state of Ireland in the first half of the twentieth century I will have failed to make clear the outstandingly obvious thing about the development of a national mind—the amazing slowness of the process, especially when, as in Ireland, isolation has ossified mental habits for a long period and unrest has subsequently made development impossible. The greatest curse of Ireland has not been English invasions or English misgovernment; it has been the exaggeration of Irish virtues —our stubbornness, conservatism, enormous arrogance, our power of resistance, our capacity for taking punishment, our laughter, endurance, fatalism, devotion to the past, all taken to that point where every human quality can become a vice instead of a virtue. So that, for example, humour becomes cynicism, endurance beçomes exhaustion, arrogance blindness and the Patriot a Blimp. In other words Ireland is learning, as Americans say, the hard way. She is like a brilliant but arrogant boy whose very brilliance acts as a dam against experience; who learns everything quickly, except experience. Our Nationalism has been our Egoism. It was our lovely, shining youth. Like all the appurtenances of youth it was lovely in its day. After its day is passed to attempt to wear it is a form of 'Death in Venice,' a middle-aged man raddling his cheeks to keep his youthful glow in times of plague. Ireland has clung to her youth, indeed to her childhood,

longer and more tenaciously than any other country in
Europe, resisting Change, Alteration, Reconstruction to
the very last. The result is often a Muddle and a Mess.

Two Problems: Provincialism . . .

The two main problems, then, facing Irish writers to-day
are Provincialism and Nationalism. I spoke just now of the
things Ireland has not got. American readers will be fully
aware of the implications, for did not Henry James, in
writing of Nathaniel Hawthorne, in order to underline the
provincialism of Hawthorne's New England, draw up a
list of the things America had not then got.

'. . . no State, in the European sense of the word, and indeed barely a specific national name. No sovereign, no
court, no personal loyalty, no aristocracy, no church, no
clergy, no army, no diplomatic service, no country gentlemen, no palaces, no castles, nor manors nor old country-
houses, nor parsonages, nor thatched cottages nor ivied
ruins; no cathedrals nor abbeys, nor little Norman churches;
no great Universities nor public schools—no Oxford, nor
Eton, nor Harrow; no literature, no novels, no museums,
no pictures, no political society, no sporting class—no Ep-
som nor Ascot!'

(What was left? James asked. Howells, in reviewing his
Hawthorne replied, 'why simply the whole of life.') What
James was getting at, however, was that Hawthorne was
much restricted by the *poverty* of life in his America. There
was not enough *interesting* life to write about. And an Irish
Henry James, also feeling that urbanity and intelligence
and institutions are necessary things to the novelist—urbanity and intelligence in his material; that is, in his char-

acters and in his milieu—might well feel also that he is immensely restricted by Irish provincialism. He might well, and indeed very reasonably, feel that if he has only peasants and peasants-in-the-towns to write about then their conflicts, their ideas, their emotions, their problems and their reactions are all frighteningly elementary.

It is undeniable. Provincial life is always compressed and inevitably limited. Realism soon exhausts the regional interest; the regional impulse soon exhausts itself. (Ireland could not produce a Henry James because it has not Henry James characters.) But as against this I warmly recommend to all Irish, and many American writers who may feel a like compression and limitation, a brilliant essay by Herbert Read on Hawthorne, in *The Sense of Glory* (Cambridge University Press) in which he points out the brighter side of this provincialism; and to appreciate which I need do no more than point to what English provincial life gave to English literature in such writers as Wordsworth, Sterne, the Brontës, Hardy, Bennett, Lawrence and others such. For there are not only many compensations in being provincial—in the best sense: there is a certain source of strength, of sanity, of common-sense, of freedom from the danger of being precious, or *chi-chi* in the provincial's closer intimacy with people. His natural wonder lives longer. The boredom of the metropolis is held longer at bay.

The dangers need no underlining. Herbert Read speaks of the writer's roots being sunk deeper in the soil where the outlook is confined, and Irish literature amply illustrates what he means; but Irish literature also illustrates what he means by the confined outlook, for this word 'soil' will readily suggest to us how soon a yawning boredom may follow the constant repetition of over-familiar peasant motifs. One need go no further than the Abbey Theatre to see how easily this repetition exhausts the soil, and our interest. Man is a thinking animal, and writers are supposed to think more intensely than other men, and when they have depicted all the usual local rural themes—land-hunger, match-making, sexual-repression, the farcical side of village-life, political jobbery, nationalist fervours and nationalist disillusions and so on—they naturally want to turn, with the turn of their thoughts, to those other issues which the world's wider stage brings to their notice. I do not mean here political issues only. I mean all sorts of issues: moral and emotional. But if the life about them is too confined or elementary to pose those questions, what can the writers do? We know well what they can do. They can do what Henry James did—follow the interest of their thoughts to other lands. They do what Shaw did, and Joyce, and Wilde, and O'Casey, and Elizabeth Bowen; and how many other Irish writers? They do what Arnold Bennett did, and Conrad and D. H. Lawrence, and how many other English writers? They go into exile, overwhelmed by the thought that struck James, 'that the flower of art blooms only where the soil is deep, that it takes a great deal of history to produce a little literature, that it needs a complex social machinery to set a writer in motion.'

The Irish public is often puzzled by the feeling (which is entirely justified) that Irish writers are, for some reason which the public cannot understand, irritated by Irish life. But it is natural that we should be. As far as we are concerned Irish life is our material, and we naturally want it to be various, complex, aware, adventurous and interesting on as many levels as possible. We do think that it is not aware, and that, indeed, we know that it evades awareness. We see in it a good deal of moral cowardice, of timidity in the face of challenge. If we were more urbane we should treat this as the subject of comedy, and I do not fully understand why we do not do so unless it be that a certain tawdriness in the general technique of evasion repels us. The Irish public may, to give an actual example, be puzzled that Irish writers tend to be anti-clerical, as they do. Yet nobody who has read my chapter on 'The Priests' can fail to see why this should be so. After all, this is not a local thing. No Irish writer has been as indignantly anti-clerical as the Catholic novelist Bernanos; and the reasons are not dissimilar. Thus Bernanos' rage (in his *Brazilian Diary*) against the *'devots,'* what we call the pietists, is fully understandable to us who see in pietism not innocence or enthusiasm but cunning and self-interest on the part of the laity, and a bland and short-sighted self-satisfaction on the part of our priests.

That Irish writing should, in our time, become critical, and at bottom moralist, is therefore natural. That it should be angry is natural; if a great pity, for anger is not a fruitful emotion. That it ought, conversely, struggle desperately against anger and didacticism is equally evident; fight for its own ease of heart, for the lyricism and sweetness that anger and contempt would destroy; for humour, and good-humour; and, above all, for intelligence and detachment. Otherwise the social milieu will drag it down and finally choke it. There is in Irish provincialism, therefore, both good and evil from the viewpoint of writers living in Ireland. It offers them a dilemma which they must, somehow, face and solve. The same is true of that other abiding Irish emotion—an unthinking Nationalism, but this, I think, we have handled somewhat better.

. . . and Nationalism

Nationalism, according to Marx, withers away when the national ego is satisfied. Any Irishman, looking at Britain and the British Empire, could only remark, with a certain dryness, that it certainly withers very nicely into Imperialism. Any Irishman, looking about him to-day in Ireland, can only remark wearily that Nationalism is an appetite that grows by what it feeds on. I see no signs of a withering of Irish Nationalism but I record with satisfaction that it has bloated into xenophobia and chauvinism, and that what devoured Irish literature a hundred years ago is precisely what is vainly attempting to choke it to-day. I say it 'with satisfaction' because the great difference between a normal patriotism and a dropsical chauvinism is not so much that the one is healthy and the other is a disease as that the one is common property and the other is private property; by which I mean that I do not believe that patriotism is the last refuge of a scoundrel, but I do believe that chauvinism is, and although I have never studied the life of the original Sergeant Chauvin, who caused himself to be lowered into the grave by knotted tricolours, I should be greatly surprised if he did not also climb in the world under cover of the flag. Nationalism does not wither away, there are always too many people eager to water it with their tears and harvest its dividends with a smile. What happens is that when the true patriot has done his necessary work he carelessly leaves the Tree of Liberty to every crook and scamp who comes in his wake, and they, being false priests, neglect it and abuse it. The Tree of Liberty is not a thing of nature, it is a work of art, a much-grafted and tended plant, and when the faux-patriot gets it the old stock shoots up from below the graft, the scion dies, and you get nasty little crabs instead of 'the apple-tree, the singing and the gold.'

We will always find true and unassuming and selfless patriots, in Ireland, and England, and every country in the world; but we will recognise them only in times of crisis, such as war, when patriotism is an expensive virtue; less often in times of peace when patriotism is profitable. Now that Ireland has achieved her Peace she has no temptation to exploit any other country under cover of 'patriotism,' but there are great temptations to Irishmen to exploit one another under cover of 'patriotism,' and pietism and goodness, and sweetness, and purity, and innocence, and the devil only knows what other hypocrisy; and small but virulent numbers of them have been doing this for the last twenty-five years. Since the last stage of a disease is always the worst one welcomes the foulness of chauvinism, would have it, indeed, get worse and worse until it kills its victim. Blimpism, Jingoism, and all such impostures, were not killed in Britain until they reached their peak of folly, and a peak it was, a Capitoline Hill, to which the old guard retreated step by step waving the flag more and more wildly as commonsense and human decency pursued them. When Shaw was attacking them in England in the Preface to *John Bull's Other Island* nobody, they least of all, paid any attention to him; and the domination of the politician by the militarist not only went on, unnoticed, but probably still goes on though now in a greatly attenuated way. They do not die badly, these ruffians, and they die slowly.

If, then, chauvinism is still powerful in Ireland to-day, as it still is, and will probably go on being for a long time to come, it is not because it is widespread—it is not—but because it is the racket of the powerful few, and this one welcomes because to have arrived at a stage where the true patriotism, as the property of the many, and this false patriotism as the property of the few, thus clearly define themselves is to have arrived at that civilised state of tension when men of reason can at last appeal, in the name of a sensible and possible and decent and tolerable concept of nationality, not to the few against the many as it was in the days of Ireland's slavery, but to the many against the few in these days of her liberation.

This, at least, Irish writers have done: they have forced a concentration of power to expose itself, they have in part defined the conflict. The groups take shape—liberals, chauvinists, bureaucrats, pietists, professional peasants, native middle-classes, the frank and brutal racketeers, 'friends,' 'enemies,' tensions that are at last intelligible and recognisable. The enemy (however each group thinks of it) is no longer external; so that every Englishman now visiting Ireland has the pleasant experience of being received with open arms as a 'friendly neutral,' and will either be told not of the perfidies of John Bull but of the wickednesses of Paddy Citizen, or be told nothing at all except the latest joke or gossip, and so, entertained with laughter and, blessedly unaware of subterranean conflicts, he will leave behind him the most good-humoured country in the world.

But writers are only voices, and history is a process, and the thoughts which are its events are not so much thought-up as hammered into mortal heads. I have quoted the late R. G. Collingwood at the beginning of this book —'History proper is the history of thought; there are no mere events in history.' He goes on to say that these seeming events are actions that express some thought, or intention, or purpose of their agents, and that the historian's job is to identify the thought behind the act. But he also says that 'many' actions, or *actiones,* are really *passiones,* or the things that men endure. Instead of the word 'many' should he not here have put 'most,' and then made some synthesis with the reactions from these experiences that we endure—and by which, if we have any capacity at all for abstracting from our experiences, we also learn? That is all I have tried to do. That is what Ireland must do. Is she doing it? I think so. If Ireland has endured much, and has in the long view of history as yet learned little by experience and that slowly, she *has* learned. She will, painfully, learn more. That, I regard as the finest tribute any man can pay to any country. My only wish for Ireland is that she might try to learn a little more quickly in the future than she has done in the past. And the non-Irish reader may well think that it is rather selfish of me to confine that wish to my own country.